# David Lilienthal

## Public Servant in a Power Age

# David Lilienthal
## Public Servant in a Power Age

by WILLSON WHITMAN

26/28

NEW YORK: HENRY HOLT AND COMPANY

FIRST PRINTING

## ACKNOWLEDGMENTS

BECAUSE this book is not a biography, but the story of a man's work in public service as it appears to a member of the public, its sources are not in private records but in public documents. Chief contributor is the Government Printing Office, with the Technical Library of the Tennessee Valley Authority at Knoxville providing its usual help.

Thanks in particular are due to Dr. J. H. Rush of the Federation of American Scientists, Washington, for valuable corrections on proofs; to Randall Rubenstein, New York, both for suggesting the book and for patient editorial advice; and to Miss Valerie Reich, Central Park West, the world's most conscientious typist.

Lines from "Atomic Power," the song by Fred Kirby, are copyrighted by the Leeds Music Corporation and reprinted here by permission of the copyright owner. The TVA song is from *Ballad Makin' in the Mountains of Kentucky* by Jean Thomas (copyright, 1939, by Henry Holt and Company, Inc.). Material from *The Progressive Farmer* is quoted by courtesy of that magazine.

The letter from President Roosevelt to Representative Estes Kefauver is published with the consent of the executors of the Roosevelt estate.

# David Lilienthal

## Public Servant in a Power Age

I

*"This, in a true sense, is a return to the spirit and vision of the pioneer."*

FRANKLIN DELANO ROOSEVELT,
Message to Congress asking establishment of the Tennessee Valley Authority.

ON JULY 6, 1933, a young man swung off Southern Train Number 17, climbed the stairs of the Knoxville depot and looked out over tracks and viaducts to see which way was town. He had an important day ahead: the directors of the Tennessee Valley Authority were to have their first meeting in the Valley.

That summer the United States, a big and normally rich nation, was up to its neck in the private business of selling apples on the public streets. To Knoxville this was nothing new. They had always sold apples and other produce at the farmers' market in the center of town, where, since the War Between the States, apple growers and sellers of field peas and turnip greens and sweet potatoes suffered the hard times familiar to farm folk in an industrial world. Not enough money changed hands to pay for hogback to cook with the greens, or flour for biscuits in sacks to cut into clothes for the children.

Knoxville is on the Tennessee River where it starts

[ 1 ]

flowing west from the Smoky Mountains. Indians in that region used to say that a big turkey buzzard, lighting on an island in the oxbow bend of the river just below Lookout Mountain, flapped his wings twice and made the Tennessee Valley. Knoxville is in the depression made by the east wing. And in 1933 Knoxville was sure enough in a depression, with the buzzard sitting ready for the carcass.

Joined to the nation in mutual misery, the long-remembering people of Tennessee had to suffer one more invasion by government forces from the North. According to an Act of the 73rd Congress, the Tennessee Valley Authority was created "for the purpose of maintaining and operating the properties now owned by the United States in the vicinity of Muscle Shoals, Alabama, in the interest of the national defense and for agricultural and industrial development, and to improve navigation in the Tennessee River and to control the destructive flood waters in the Tennessee River and Mississippi River basins."

In Knoxville people didn't see how all this could be done. The story was that the New Dealers planned to dam the river at Cove Creek and increase the power output down at the Shoals, but why would they want more electric power when people couldn't pay for what they had?

The government was serious, though, because Washington took Dr. Harcourt A. Morgan, president of the University of Tennessee, away from his job to be one of the three men to run TVA. The chairman of the board was another man of the same name, but no relation—Dr. Arthur Morgan, from Ohio. Dr. Arthur Morgan was an engineer who had built flood-control dams up in Ohio and over in Arkansas; he was also head of Antioch College. Nobody in Knoxville knew the third member of the board, a Mr. David Lilienthal, who came in on the train from way up in Wisconsin.

The other two directors were already in Knoxville. Dr. H. A. Morgan lived there, and the chairman had come early to get things started. When you saw Dr. Arthur Morgan, if you were any judge of character you knew that here was a man who would be capable of going right ahead by himself without help from anybody. He looked, thought, and acted like a leader; nearing sixty, he was still full of vigor, and a crest of gray hair above his hawklike face only added to the impressiveness of his appearance. He could have been a general or an admiral, an actor or a preacher with a big personal following. In a way that is what he was, because Antioch College trained its students in Christian ethics, and Dr. Morgan inspired sincere admiration there.

In a quieter way, the Tennessee Morgan had his own well-established reputation over the whole South. The University wasn't just a higher-education school; it was a land-grant college with an extension service that got down to earth and helped the farmers, working with the county agents over the state. Dr. H. A. Morgan was a famous agronomist and entomologist who knew the problems of dirt farmers from Tennessee to Texas. Ten years older than Dr. Arthur Morgan, Dr. H. A. Morgan was one of those lean, stringy, sandy-haired, lantern-jawed individuals who never show age. He wasn't the sort to talk too

[ 3 ]

much, either, which may have been why the farmers trusted him.

Dr. Arthur Morgan would build the dams and Dr. H. A. Morgan, people supposed, was on the board to make Tennessee put up with the whole thing. Mr. Lilienthal was a lawyer by profession and it was assumed that he would have to do with TVA land purchase. He was a slight, serious-looking young man, ruddy and fair skinned, with hazel eyes behind the shell-rimmed glasses. In the spring a White House telegram had called him home from a fishing trip to meet Dr. Arthur Morgan in Chicago, and as the chairman said later, "I found a direct, open young man, candid, just the picture of candor and young enthusiasm."

Actually David Lilienthal was thirty-four, but people always thought he was younger. When the Knoxville press assembled to meet him a reporter asked him for a pencil, under the impression that the man they were here to interview was some sort of office boy. But the President knew what he was doing when he put Lilienthal on the TVA board.

Moving fast the way some first-generation American boys do to use the advantages that their fathers crossed the ocean to give them, David Lilienthal graduated from high school in Michigan City, Indiana, at seventeen and from DePauw University at twenty-one. Too good at extempore debate to go to work in the family store, at twenty-three he had a law degree from Harvard. His father, who had started in to be a citizen when he started to learn English, the day he landed, was happy about this choice of career.

[ 4 ]

There were three boys, David, Theodore—named for the first President Roosevelt—and Allen. As the oldest, David at six made a New York trip with his father. A big round straw hat on the back of David's young head, they look solemn but happy in a photograph taken in one of those goat-drawn carriages they had in city parks for children to ride in.

Sharing his father's respect for the government of the United States, young David specialized in public-service law. Admitted to the bar in Illinois, he started practice in Donald Richberg's Chicago office, handling labor cases and also litigation for the city of Chicago. With other lawyers he worked on and helped win for the public a famous rate case—Smith vs. Illinois Bell Telephone Company—that required a six-hundred-page brief, and arguments before the Supreme Court. Later he distinguished himself in a case involving the railway labor act, so that before he opened his own office the young lawyer's reputation among other lawyers was made. He edited a series of reports on utilities, served as secretary of the American Bar Association standing committee on public utilities law, and lectured on the subject at Northwestern University.

No doubt a smart young lawyer could make more in other fields, or anyhow on the corporation side. But, although he was married by now and had two small children, Nancy Alice and David Junior, Lilienthal knew what he wanted to do. His wife wasn't one to hold him back. Helen Marian Lamb, a fellow student at DePauw, had early decided that this Lilienthal boy showed promise.

[ 5 ]

By campus standards he had, indeed, already arrived. From top grades in high school he was a certainty for Phi Beta Kappa; also he was on the football squad and starred in school plays, worked on the student paper and the annual, and helped organize the journalism fraternity. In between he did a little light heavyweight boxing and was for two years president of the student body. Pretty Helen Lamb was another good student, and the combination of brains with blue eyes and dark wavy hair, sympathetic mouth and firm chin entitled her to the attention of any boy as bright as Dave Lilienthal.

Her people were movers too. They'd come over earlier, when New England and Virginia were first settled, and moved first to Indiana, then to Oklahoma in time to give Helen a chance to say she was born in the South. She went back to Indiana for college and, after DePauw, a curious coincidence led her to do postgraduate work at Radcliffe while Dave Lilienthal went into Felix Frankfurter's law class at Harvard. But Helen wasn't a career girl; on marrying Dave, she made his career her concern. She teased him about marrying money because her first salary as an English teacher was more than his as a beginning lawyer. But she would never hold him back. She was willing to live in Chicago or Timbuktu if Dave said go.

Another move was coming. When Governor Philip La Follette of Wisconsin undertook to reorganize the state railroad commission into a new public utilities commission, he first asked Lilienthal to write the new law and then appointed him to be one of the three commissioners. When he left Chicago for Wisconsin, members of the local

[ 6 ]

bar gave the thirty-two-year-old Lilienthal a farewell dinner at the Union League Club. The only trouble was
that, wearing a black tie and wing collar, he still looked
like an honor graduate.

In Wisconsin, a two years' fight was ahead. In a flush of
legislative reform, the laws asked for by Lilienthal and
the son of "Fighting Bob" had been passed. Some people
couldn't see why the Governor had to go outside the state
to find a commissioner; or why, building up an effective
regulatory body, the commission hired more experts from
outside and brought in college professors from New York
to testify at rate hearings. But the Governor knew what he
wanted; he and Lilienthal had talked all night, making
plans. The Insull scandal, breaking, suggested that something should be done; Lilienthal's proposal was for regulation to be simplified and speeded up. "You see, I have
a very strong feeling that if we cannot control our basic
industries, and certainly nothing is more basic than the
utilities industry, then we have no government in fact,
merely a pathetic fiction of government."

The alternate to control was, of course, public ownership. Wisconsin was not deaf to discussion of the subject.
In a speech made two months after he went to Madison the
new commissioner told the Wisconsin Municipal Utilities
Association, "I would like to emphasize that the future of
public ownership of electric utilities cannot depend merely
upon emotion, upon resentment of the abuses of private
ownership, upon sentiment and generalizations. There
must be knowledge, technical skill and receptivity to new
ideas."

[ 7 ]

With farm and factory earnings way down, while some utilities dividends stayed up as high as 12 per cent, there was bound to be resentment of utilities rates. As milk prices fell lower Wisconsin farmers held meetings at the capitol to protest the high cost of electricity. Lilienthal thought the farm use of electric power should be charged at the low industrial rate.

More, in his rate case against the Wisconsin Telephone Company Lilienthal suggested that "The company should give some weight to the fact that there has been a substantial increase in the purchasing power of the dollar paid to the Wisconsin Telephone Company in the form of rates, and in the dollar paid by it to the American Telephone and Telegraph Company in the form of dividends." The papers came right out and said that even with purchasing power high a Milwaukee phone exchange spent $1,938 for linoleum and $859 in "engineering costs" to lay it. The public was paying not only for the linoleum but for the entertainment of state legislators, and officials' club dues in the depression year 1932 amounting to more than $18,000.

By the end of the second year in Wisconsin the new commission had ordered utilities rate reductions estimated to save 420,000 consumers an annual total of $2,350,000, one million of this a reduction in freight rates. Also arguing that it was the duty of the commission to protect investors as well as consumers, Lilienthal said Insull subsidiaries in Wisconsin would not be drained for the benefit of holding company receiverships. This, the papers said, was "the first time a state commission has stepped in to protect investors and consumers in a receivership action."

But the utilities were fighting back, carrying injunction suits clear to the Supreme Court at Washington. Meanwhile the utilities commission was a big issue in the state election. It was being described as "one of the most forceful regulatory bodies in the country," and other states were copying the Wisconsin laws. Wisconsin, said a Chicago editorial, was "one of the few states whose public-service commission in recent years has functioned with complete independence and fidelity to the public interest, and in reasonable conformity with settled principles bearing upon the regulation of public utilities." President Roosevelt, speaking in Milwaukee, praised the work of the commission. The winning candidate for governor was pledged to reappoint Lilienthal, but there were suggestions that the state senate might not confirm. Balky legislators were considering a bill to separate his carefully assembled staff experts from their jobs, by depriving of civil service rights any state employee not a resident of Wisconsin for six months before appointment.

There were guesses that Lilienthal would return to profitable private practice, or be appointed by the President to the Federal Power Commission. The President, as it happened, had other plans. With Senator Norris, he had been considering a project in the Tennessee Valley that would combine Norris' long fight for public power at Muscle Shoals with Roosevelt's own wish to do something for that third of the nation that was worst housed, worst clothed, and worst fed.

[ 9 ]

Dr. Arthur Morgan's appointment to the new Authority board was announced first, then Dr. H. A. Morgan's. The Lilienthal appointment when it came brought no excitement to the Valley but caused some in Wisconsin. The papers pointed out that, as utilities corporations "just naturally do not like a man who knows how to probe their affairs," they had been "moving heaven and earth to get Lilienthal out of the Wisconsin picture." Three big battles were still going on. But the papers noted, "The United States government will enjoy his services without even asking where he was born."

After his appointment but before he reached the South, rates were cut in the territory of the Tennessee Electric Power Company. So young Mr. Lilienthal might have been excused for being a little self-conscious or prideful when he got to Tennessee; but he wasn't.

At that first meeting in the Knoxville Chamber of Commerce, with the two directors from the North sweltering in white suits while Dr. H. A. Morgan looked dry and cool in a dark one, Dr. Arthur Morgan as chairman naturally took things in hand. He told reporters, afterward, about his plans for the Valley—he hoped for small industry of the sort they had in France, to supplement agriculture. If Tennessee farmers should make their own shoes, for example, it "wouldn't hurt existing shoe factories because they don't sell many shoes to these people anyhow." This wasn't the most tactful thing to say in Knoxville, where they had shoe stores, or even in any part of the South where they have long been sensitive about whether or not enough shoes are worn. Dr. Arthur reassured the reporters by going on to say that the Authority "would not prohibit mass production," but talk about prohibiting any kind of industry, in the South in 1933, sounded queer.

Mr. Lilienthal, the reporters noted, asked a lot of questions but spoke only briefly: "I am greatly interested in two things, people and facts. The purpose of this project, as far as I am concerned, is to make the people happier. I am terribly interested now in finding out more facts about the Tennessee Valley."

To learn more facts young Mr. Lilienthal took a trip through the Valley with Dr. H. A. Morgan, while Dr. Arthur went off to address the Tennessee Press Association at Redboiling Springs. Going down the river young David introduced himself to the people he met: "I'm the director who isn't named Morgan, and isn't a college president, and hasn't got a doctor's degree."

There were welcoming receptions and banquets all down the line, and Lilienthal smiled and waved a panama at his new neighbors, but they observed that he made no definite commitments about where dams would be built, or when power could be transmitted to the communities that were asking for it. This caution won Southern respect and the papers reported that preliminary negotiations were progressing.

It was September before Mr. Lilienthal made any major speeches in his new territory. One of the first was a difficult assignment; he had to break the bad news to the Rotary Club at Chattanooga that there would be some delay in the building of Chickamauga dam, Wheeler dam in Alabama being authorized by the President to follow Norris. This was a disappointment to Chattanooga, caught between two centers of Valley development, and needing the construction at Chickamauga to solve the unemployment problem. It was a letdown comparable to what a country counting on quick application of atomic power might now feel on being told that such hopes are premature. And the Lilienthal speech, dealing with long-range objectives and methods of public power development, has a present significance:

This capacity to produce enough for all of us, which holds such a great hope for a future high standard of living, has been made possible, in large part, by electric power. And we are just at the beginning of this power age. The future possibilities are as limitless as the practical imagination of our scientists and the ingenuity of our inventors.

No wonder, then, that it is so vital that we maintain the strictest public control over this great natural resource. The public must protect its interest in so vital a force.

Public operation, said Mr. Lilienthal, was being tried because commission regulation had proved inadequate. But he insisted that Congress had not "declared a national policy against the private ownership and operation of public utilities." The TVA power program was a constructive measure:

If the resources of this Valley are developed and stimulated through this program which Congress has set up, then every one in the Valley will benefit from it, and among the beneficiaries will, of course, be those corporations engaged in the sale of electric power; for the demand for power, obviously, will greatly increase with an increase in industrial activity and an increase in the economic well-being of the people of the Valley.

Beginning like a good Southerner to talk history, Mr. Lilienthal noted that development of the river was no new idea in Tennessee. He mentioned Andrew Jackson, Sam Houston, and Cordell Hull. And he brought down the house when he answered—with a reminder of Insull—disparaging remarks made by the Chicago *Tribune* about political handouts to the hill folk of Tennessee.

His hearers liked it when he told them:

The Tennessee Valley Authority power program is not a taxpayers' subsidy. It is a business undertaking.

You are businessmen. Many of you are manufacturers just as we are. We are both obligated to operate our business on a sound basis.

They even continued to like it when he went on:

As a manufacturer, you would consider as most unsound any suggestion that you double the capacity of your plant, even if your bank would advance the money, unless you were pretty sure that you would be able to develop a market for the increased product by the time the plant addition was completed. Rightly so, you would be most critical of us were we to do the same thing.

This put extension of the power program in the direction of Chattanooga fairly and squarely up to Chattanooga

[ 13 ]

citizens, and they got the idea. There is a certain parallel between this early TVA speech, telling the people of the Valley that the sharing of positive benefits depended on their own action, and a speech made by Lilienthal to the Atomic Energy Commission of the United Nations, nearly fourteen years later, in which he warned that action by the nations would determine the extent to which they could expect to share in United States development of atomic power.

When he approached the theoretical side at Chattanooga, Lilienthal was very careful to emphasize that he was preaching a brand of idealism that was hardheaded. The long-range aims were there:

Those who believe that things as they are cannot be improved will wonder why we should be concerned with a better planning of economic and social life. But those with a sense of humility, who see all about them want in the midst of plenty —factories idle while men need their products which the manufacturers want to produce—millions of farmers desperate because they have produced too much while other millions of men go hungry for lack of these very crops—those who see these distressing facts and are puzzled and troubled by them will join in any intelligent effort to bring a bit more of order into a world which so desperately cries out for it.

But the Lilienthal recommendations were practical. Commenting, the *News,* a Chattanooga daily favorable to TVA, said, "To be convincing, a public speaker must have knowledge of his subject, and must have power of words and personality. Mr. Lilienthal convinced the audience of 300

[ 14 ]

leaders in business and professional life that he spoke with authority. And they accepted his speech, even though it contained some disappointment for ardent Chickamauga dam supporters, as gracefully as he rendered it." The Chattanooga *Times,* strongly opposed at this period to all that TVA stood for, nevertheless approved the hardheaded approach: "No idle dreamer is Mr. Lilienthal, youngest of the three directors."

At Memphis the audience was bigger and the result similar. Mr. Lilienthal played golf with his Rotary hosts, then, in the political center of Tennessee, quoted freely from President Roosevelt, to whose bandwagon Boss Crump was clinging. In his speech of introduction Senator McKellar, doing the same, made a small error of date and referred to President Theodore Roosevelt; he did better when he turned from the past to describe Lilienthal as "a young man with a great future before him."

Lilienthal repeated one sentence from the Chattanooga speech that was to become a byword: "The Tennessee Valley project is an opportunity and a challenge to the people of the South." As at Chattanooga, he talked about immediate and long-range programs, and emphasized the need for joint action by local agencies if any program was to succeed. He was reassuring about power:

The Authority is not engaged in a punitive expedition against the utilities. The Authority is an instrument of the people of the United States. It is charged with the duty of carrying out a national power policy. . . . But in carrying it out, the Authority is determined to bring the least possible injury to actual investments in useful property.

[ 15 ]

Speaking at Nashville in November, Lilienthal was able to report real progress at Norris dam. He could also describe the new contract with Tupelo, Mississippi, the first town to have TVA power, with a saving of more than sixty per cent over the old rates. He talked in some detail about the utilities fight, bringing it home by quoting Federal Trade Commission findings about advertising in the Tennessee papers, and making the point that small investors as well as consumers had lost money.

Meanwhile Dr. Arthur Morgan was making speeches too, in the Valley and to planners or to academic groups in the North. Dr. Arthur Morgan could talk with clearness, charm, and logic about abstract issues and some practical details. But a young lawyer who had already had considerable experience in public administration must have squirmed to hear the chairman's vague good words for the Italian, the German, and the Russian systems; his assurance to Valley folks that the Authority would borrow the best from these systems. Valley people just didn't hold with taking anything from foreigners. So if David Lilienthal and Dr. H. A. Morgan listened with misgivings when Dr. Arthur Morgan spoke for the board, they had with them large numbers of the people in Knoxville, at Chattanooga, up in the hills and down at the Shoals.

The President had spoken of "a return to the spirit and vision of the pioneer." There was no doubt that in Dr. Arthur Morgan the pioneer spirit was strong; he wanted to establish a new and better world, he had the will, and he thought he saw the way to do it. He had a good deal of the righteous confidence that shone in the settlement of New England, or in the Mormon settlement of Utah.

But America has come to recognize two sets of pioneers—those who landed early at Plymouth Rock or Jamestown, and those who came later and kept coming. It is natural for the older strain, brushing aside such errors as Cotton Mather made, to feel itself in all ways superior—as natural as it was for Dr. Arthur Morgan, as chairman of TVA, to assume a primacy over his fellow directors. To settle the dispute it is perhaps necessary to consider what values actually help the survival of a new settlement. Among the useful traits, the determination—not to say stubborn self-righteousness—of the early Puritan settlers looms large. But in time other qualities became essential to survival. Among these the ability to withstand attack and adapt to new but natural conditions can be as important as the will to establish a predetermined order.

The new Authority, if not completely surrounded by enemies, had to be careful not to make any more than were already there. The seven Valley states were ready to welcome a project with millions to spend, but as a matter of course the politicians of those states expected to have a say-so about what was done with the money. The act had been drawn to give the Authority "the flexibility of a private corporation," but the private corporations sometimes consulted in a friendly way with Southern politicians. At any rate the politicians expected to recommend people for jobs. But already, in Wisconsin, David Lilienthal had developed his own ideas about how to find and keep good people. He wasn't likely to see eye to eye on employment with Senator McKellar of Tennessee, or Congressman May of Kentucky, or even Congressman Rankin of Mississippi, who had worked hard for TVA.

[ 17 ]

Besides the problem of getting on with state politicians, there was an outside threat. In Wisconsin, Lilienthal had found that state regulation of utilities was difficult because you had to deal with holding companies operating on a national scale. In the Valley you had a bigger field; not one state but a whole river region. And the holding company, Commonwealth and Southern, was bigger still, and a customer of the government—the little trickle of electricity produced at Muscle Shoals by the original Wilson dam was under contract to a privately owned distributing system which, traced through, had its headquarters up in Delaware. Already the president of the holding company, Wendell Willkie, had said what he thought of TVA.

Had the Tennessee Valley Authority been a relief or improvement project, like WPA or the CCC camps, it must have vanished as those projects did vanish. As a power development it could go on functioning only by growing strong. The program was complex—that was why the President had talked to Senator Norris about David Lilienthal before he made the appointment with Dr. Arthur Morgan in Chicago. Lilienthal's job would be very difficult if strained relations with the people of the Valley should add to the hazards in the power fight.

Dr. H. A. Morgan also needed good relations if he was to persuade farmers to use the phosphate fertilizer which the Authority's electric power could produce. He would deal not alone with the hill folk, but with farm people all the way down into Alabama, some of them definitely set against the ways of the hills. Dr. H. A. Morgan couldn't see imposing any stringent social reforms on Alabama

[ 18 ]

farmers. He could see a wide and helpful distribution of phosphates if he could tie in all the existing agencies, local, state, and federal, rather than work against them in an independent setup. As a first move in co-operation Dr. H. A. Morgan already had in his hands the kingpiece, the University of Tennessee and its farm-extension system which was tied in with the county agents and was a successful going concern held in respect.

On certain matters before the directors there was, fortunately, real agreement. One problem concerned the central office of the Authority, which the Act assumed would be at Muscle Shoals. For different reasons, the directors all preferred Knoxville. Dr. H. A. Morgan lived there and the university activities centered there. Lilienthal, shuttling back and forth to Washington or New York on power business, could save time by not traveling the length of the Valley. Dr. Arthur was building a dam at Norris and while there would be down-river dams, he would always prefer the hills. It was to be hoped that he wouldn't continue to rebuke the Shoals people too severely for their attempts to start a real estate boom.

About another matter there was complete, enthusiastic, and lasting agreement: the Authority's refusal to consider political recommendations in hiring people. Dr. Arthur was most vocal about this, but every one of the directors had occasion to explain it to the hungry politicians of seven states. Fourteen years later, David Lilienthal was to look a United States senator in the eye and say, "I think you and I understood one another about that, Senator, at our first meeting."

In September the Lilienthal family had arrived in

Tennessee. In the spring, Mrs. Lilienthal had stayed on in Wisconsin to dispose of the house there, then had taken the children to spend the summer with their grandparents. Later their father went to Indiana and drove the family down in time to get settled before school started.

Norris houses were still at a premium; so the first Lilienthal address was Knoxville, a brick house on Melrose Place near the university. The children started school, Nancy in the fourth grade though she was only eight, and David, five, ready for the second grade before Tennessee schools expected him at all. There started the story of "David's I.Q." which was to follow and annoy him through his school life.

Both children needed their I.Q.'s for adjustment to Southern schools. Mrs. Lilienthal worried a little because Nancy's school building had been condemned as unsafe. But Nancy and David found themselves answering a barrage of childish questions: "What's your name? Who is your father? What does he do? What church do you go to?" and answering wrong. The answers in themselves were all right: Lilienthal, and it's easy to spell if you know how, as easy as Sevier or Stooksbury. My father works for TVA —not WPA, the Tennessee Valley Authority. My mother's a Presbyterian. Only the accent was wrong; Nancy, who spent the seven formative years up North, complains to this day that she can't talk Southern. There was no denying that the young Lilienthals were at a disadvantage in Knoxville. Of course, it wasn't their fault that they were born that way, but there was no getting round it. They were half Yankee.

## II

*My name is William Edwards*
*I live down Cove Creek way.*
*I'm working on the project*
*They call the TVA.*
*The Government begun it*
*When I was but a child*
*And now they are in earnest*
*And Tennessee's gone wild.*

American Folksong, 1935.

ON COVE CREEK they began work on a mass of concrete that was to rise higher than Niagara Falls. In order to hire more people they used three shifts, day and night, and so TVA dam building began as it was to end, by working around the clock—first to end the depression blamed on the first World War, and last to speed construction at Fontana dam in the second World War.

The little town named for Senator Norris also took shape, and although it was never big enough to house more than a few of the people working on the dam, it was a symbol of better living conditions to come. With dam building and town building and construction orders, and offices spreading out into vacant space on Union Avenue, Knoxville began to realize that TVA was a solid asset. In a year, business was better in some fields than it had been before the depression. And Wheeler dam, down in Alabama, would spread the TVA construction program clear across the Valley.

Here was visible achievement, undoubtedly beneficial, but unless you felt like a fairy godparent you wanted to see it tied into some productive activity so that it would last. A dam for flood control alone was good but negative—like the small barriers the CCC boys were building to stop erosion. The natural function of the controlled river was to provide power, the power dreamed of by Norris and Edison and Ford and everybody who had ever looked with an enterprising eye at the Shoals.

Power production was specified in the Act and recognized from the start as part of the TVA plan; that, David Lilienthal knew, was why he was there. His job was to justify the expense of the building program by selling the product that would pay for it. In the end, increased farm earnings and new industries would return the investment, in terms of the nation's over-all economy; but the first profits to be made, and paid back to the taxpayer, would come from power sales.

As in any selling program, there would be competition. While the shovels dug into the mountain, cofferdams diverted the creek and concrete was poured in the visible operations of TVA building, a tougher struggle started among the unseen powers of the business world for the profits of this earthly activity.

It was in fact the legal contention that holding companies with headquarters in the North had active corporate bodies operating in the Valley, already occupying the space into which TVA had come. Under the right of eminent domain the government could condemn a man's farm, forcing him to move off land to be flooded by a reservoir. But to move a pole belonging to the Tennessee Electric Light and Power Company required complicated legal proceedings involving that Fourteenth Amendment to the Constitution which, designed to free the persons of Negro slaves, set up in the whole country as well as in the South a network of corporations with sensitive personal claims. Up in New York the smartest corporation lawyer of them all, Wendell Willkie, knew enough to harp on the notion that his company was a physical entity to be hurt. He talked about TVA as a threat to "dismember" and destroy. The Congressional decision to invest a little public money in public power was a "cruel" attack.

Willkie opened fire even before TVA had made any moves, because he realized that any public power program was a real threat to private exploitation. It was true that when TVA rates were announced—low, though not as low as the Tacoma rates—utilities stocks slumped on Wall Street. But TVA at the start offered no actual competition and could not until the dams were finished. The small amount of power already generated at the Shoals, there sold to the Alabama Power Company and resold to local consumers at more than thirty times its cost, could be reclaimed by TVA as the contract expired; and new lines could be built in territory where the private companies had refused service. This small beginning was no more than a sample showing of what TVA could do.

However, Lilienthal saw it as a chance to demonstrate the basic premise of cheap power, that low price increases use. So in the first tiny TVA area, around the Shoals and over as far as Tupelo, Mississippi, modern publicity put on a campaign of education in the use of stoves, refrigerators, and washing machines that could have taught the utilities corporations more than it taught the farmers. As rates went down, consumption went up, and Lauderdale county bought gadgets as well as current with an abandon equaled only by the happy share croppers of "Finian's Rainbow." When General Wood of Sears, Roebuck made a trip down to see why sales were so high, he called the TVA program "magnificent." As a farseeing manufacturer put it, "The TVA is the grandest piece of promotion that has ever broken for the electrical industry. Imagine the President of the United States standing up and saying that every home in America ought to be completely electrified!"

The Southern utilities were doing well too, their rates lowered to meet TVA competition resulting in increased business and bigger earnings. But the holding companies saw trouble ahead. TVA didn't sell current retail, but made contracts with municipally owned distribution plants, or rural co-operatives. To the little towns at the Shoals, and to cities like Knoxville and Chattanooga, PWA loans were promised for plant construction, but this the holding companies saw as unfair government competition: in bringing in outside capital for construction, Uncle Sam acted just like a holding company.

In Southern courts it was easy to enjoin the whole program and the corporations, through their local stockholders, promptly did so. By one Alabama court, fourteen small towns were blocked in their plans for using TVA power. Local people who were for TVA complained that courts, banks, and papers were dominated by the Alabama Power Company. The city of Birmingham, in fact, voted against using TVA power because of a fear that company headquarters would be moved if bonds were voted to build a municipal plant. Other cities, Knoxville and Memphis and Chattanooga, were for TVA but were deprived of cheap power while negotiations to buy out company-owned plants were endlessly prolonged.

The pattern of the struggle was repeated all over the Valley: TVA would be welcomed with whoops of joy by the people who wanted cheaper lights or, in the case of farmers, any kind of lights. The utilities company, waking up, would lower rates or, in dark farm country, hastily string the wires which people called "spite lines." When people persisted in wanting TVA power—which was cheaper than the lowered rates, and promised to reach the farms, four out of five even near Knoxville, that had no electricity—the answer was battle in the courts.

Lilienthal had always been in complete sympathy with the people who asked for power; back in Wisconsin, in a speech to engineers, he had said: "The change from human power to inanimate sources of power spells almost the whole difference between our civilization of today and that of a hundred years ago." To a modern mind it was wicked to see the Shoals country, recognized as a natural power source for over a century, still literally one of the darkest spots on the continent. Lilienthal called the use

[ 25 ]

of electricity in the Valley "parsimonious and niggardly."

On the other hand, he had from the first tried to keep TVA on a sound business basis, to make it a successful working enterprise rather than a social experiment. He liked using the word "bankable." He told a Washington reporter that the areas of first development were "chosen on a basis of business rather than for competitive or social reasons," and added, "If this Valley is developed as President Roosevelt's plan provides, everybody will benefit."

To make these policies clear he issued an eleven-point "Bill of Rights for power" which summarized the issues: Power is a public business, in which the public interest must prevail. But public and private interest must be reconciled whenever possible; duplication of effort and equipment must be avoided; and government enterprise must at all times be open for public inspection.

If the utilities companies chose to fight, of course he was there to fight and, as he told the Lawyers' Club in Atlanta, it would be "no Sunday school picnic."

Trying negotiation first, TVA began, through Lilienthal, a long series of meetings with Wendell Willkie of Commonwealth and Southern, intended to buy for the government first a part, then the whole of the corporation's holdings in the Valley. At the same time there were efforts to buy city distribution systems such as the one at Knoxville, owned by a local company affiliated with Electric Bond and Share. The head of that corporation, who came to Knoxville for negotiations, himself afforded a remarkable example of the duplication of effort in private utilities, since he was at one time chairman or director of forty-seven boards. Acting for Knoxville, Lilienthal refused to pay government money to "bail out the white elephant" of an unprofitable street railway, yet the bondholders admitted the price paid—par—was fair.

Meanwhile the Commonwealth and Southern negotiations took the form of legal assault. At one time thirty-seven injunction suits tried to stop TVA activity; nineteen power companies brought separate suits and then united in one long-drawn-out action headed for the Supreme Court. The best paid legal talent in the country was on the utilities side, with Newton D. Baker, Wilson's Secretary of War, as the most prominent. Lilienthal countered with a good Republican—John Lord O'Brian of Buffalo—as a special counsel for TVA.

Above and beyond the legal struggle was the political setup, with Valley politicians watching to see which way the cat would jump. In local relationships there was relatively little trouble; although individual politicians might sell out under power-company influence, city governments could see which side their bread was buttered on. Even Boss Crump of Memphis said, after the Rotary Club dinner at the Hotel Peabody, that "Mr. Lilienthal is a very capable man and he knows his business." Chattanooga staged an expensive bond election, with much name calling and a struggle fatal to one of the local papers, but TVA won. With TVA paying good money into city and state treasuries "in lieu" of taxes, there could be no objection to cheap power that would stand up under a campaign.

But every year TVA had to go to Congress for money and permission to continue its work, and state politicians

with Washington jobs were another story. Alabama sena·
tors had started opposing public power back in the days of
Senator Underwood. In 1928, Senator McKellar of Tennessee had filibustered for twenty hours against the Norris
bill of that year to develop Muscle Shoals. Later the Senator, along with Mr. Crump, supported TVA, but his favor
was always fitful though his influence on the Appropriations Committee was strong. Unremitting in his opposition to TVA, which he saw as a menace to the coal pro-
ducers of his state, was Congressman May of Kentucky.
Mr. May then was chairman of the Military Affairs Committee of the House, which passes on TVA appropriations,
and although people in the Valley were plain-spoken
enough about him, no war-contracts case then came to
mind when he called TVA "a stench in the nostrils of those
who cherish the ideals of Thomas Jefferson." With a few
notable exceptions, TVA at first had to go before Congress
without the adequate understanding of congressmen and
senators from the Valley.

The long way out of this was to build up such a strong
public sentiment that even a senator from a poll-tax state—
as the Valley states, except Kentucky, all were—would not
dare oppose TVA. This meant making the power program
attractive, but more than that it meant making other activities outlined in the Act—activities against which there was
little organized opposition—indispensable.

In determining TVA policy at the start there were, as
young Mr. Lilienthal said, two things to consider—the
facts and the people. The facts showed a poor country, run-
down and overworked land that couldn't be expected to

[ 28 ]

compete in farm production with the fat lands of the northern and western states. But through this country ran a river capable of producing great power, power for improving the run-down farms and also, eventually, for tremendous industrial production.

The people were farm folk mostly, but many of them had learned to work in mills and factories. They made good workers, from the standpoint of the employer, because they hadn't learned how to resist exploitation. Their independence was individual, not collective. A shy survival of early English folk music in the hills was no basis on which to build co-operatives. Political utopias in the Valley, inspired by such experts as Thomas Hughes and Robert Owen, had petered out. The natural result of dam building was bound to be an approach to unity with the modern industrial world. Offered a new world of hydro-electric power, the Valley folk might be glad to devote more time to singing and whittling and perhaps to political development; but the chances were that people would ask for radios, and the latest in plastics from a nice new factory. Deplorable as this might be, the democratic way is not to govern the public in such matters, but to trust education to improve popular standards. In wanting first of all cheap power to light his house, and fertilizer to improve his land, the Valley farmer only demonstrated his basic kinship with the other people of the United States.

David Lilienthal's short and simple statement of TVA purpose, "to make the people happier," might have been accepted by Dr. Arthur Morgan with certain Socratic amendments. But the Act was written in specific terms. The basic purpose, as Dr. Arthur could point out, was flood control; as he saw it, in harnessing the river for safety, the people could be lifted up like flood sufferers off a raft, into a better existence. Beyond the actual damming of the river he appeared to see the Authority as a large-scale social-service project, establishing comfort and uplift. Most of his ideas were not only ingenious but sound, granted that the purpose of the Authority was as he saw it.

But behind the Act were the men who wrote it, who had different and definite ideas. Senator Norris wanted the TVA to make Muscle Shoals work; he felt the benefits needed would follow naturally from that. He wanted the region of power to be an example for the whole country.

Roosevelt's dream was even bigger; he wanted to heal the wasted South, restore it to healthy functioning as part of the nation. To put the South firmly on its feet he wanted power, he wanted a sound balance of industry and agriculture, he wanted an energetic upsurge of popular strength. He wanted the Valley to lead the way.

With the purposes of Norris and Roosevelt, Lilienthal and Dr. H. A. Morgan agreed. So did Dr. Arthur Morgan, but he understood them and proposed to carry them out in his own fashion. And many of his plans for the Valley would in fact have defeated a broad national purpose because they were separatist plans.

Dr. Arthur Morgan even planned separately when the matter was one for the board to decide. Lilienthal was at the Shoals when he read in the paper that the important post of personnel director for the Authority was to go to a man never voted on by the directors, but picked, in all innocence, by the chairman. Dr. Arthur Morgan had never served on a three-man public board. Lilienthal's Wisconsin job had given him a thorough experience in board procedure under a capable and co-operative chairman, Theodore Kronshage. In Wisconsin it was recognized that two-thirds of a board could decide for the board, a view with which Dr. H. A. Morgan agreed; but one man, even the chairman, couldn't.

There was more to this matter of majority decision than any mere embarrassment of conflict with a well-meaning man who confused the chairmanship of a committee with direction of his own construction company or even of a small college. The issue, for the Authority, was important. How was the whole system to be built: democratically up from the bottom, or in authoritarian fashion, down from the top?

By temperament and always with the very best intentions, Dr. Arthur Morgan was an authoritarian. He had the energy of the sincere world saver, and although the plan was not his, the Tennessee Valley Authority was to him what the League of Nations was to Woodrow Wilson. He wanted the best for the Valley, but like a good old-fashioned parent he expected as a matter of course to guide the growing child. The difficulty was that the Valley was not a child but a region old in history, set in its ways and cynical in viewpoint.

Had Lilienthal and Dr. H. A. Morgan not wished for peace, and not recognized the real talents of the chairman along with his defects, they could have joined forces to defeat him utterly, at the start. Instead they worked out a

[ 31 ]

sensible division of labor. Dr. Arthur Morgan was to have charge of building dams, which included building the town of Norris, and of the education and training program planned for his construction workers. Dr. H. A. Morgan was charged with the farm and reforestation program, including erosion control, phosphate fertilizer production, and land use. To David Lilienthal went the power program; and each director was to have freedom of action in his own field. Dr. Arthur Morgan agreed. Actually he had never considered the farm and power functions of the Authority to be of primary importance.

Flood control would be taken care of by the dams, but you couldn't sit and wait for a flood to prove the worth of TVA. Navigation would be useful in time, but not at first— you could deepen the river channel, but you couldn't have shipping without boats and cargoes. The thing that could be done at once was farm improvement, and fortunately Dr. H. A. Morgan, the director concerned with agriculture, was ready to go right ahead. For forty years he had been waiting for the sort of opportunity that TVA offered, and he hadn't lost the spunk he'd had when he came to the Valley and, as Lilienthal put it, said to the farmers, "Here am I, the same sort of person you are, here to help you."

Although he'd done everything he could to make the University of Tennessee useful to the farmers, Dr. H. A. Morgan had run up against the fact well known in the South, that you can't do nothin' if you ain't got nothin' to do nothin' with. A farmer could be taught that his land needed fertilizer, but what good did that do if he couldn't lay hands on the stuff? Tell him about plugging gullies and resting tired land and maybe he couldn't afford that either. So you could stand on the river bank and watch the farms wash down to the sea. Flood control would help some, of course, if soil didn't silt up the dams as it had some of those built by the private power corporations.

As he listened to the facts about the farm situation, Lilienthal's legal mind began to work. It was like the house that Jack built. Rain fell in the Valley—Dr. H. A. Morgan always liked to start talking about rainfall, because a high rainfall made the Valley, potentially, one of the most fertile districts in the world. The rains fell, making floods to be controlled. They also washed down the fields, making necessary the use of fertilizer which hard-up farmers couldn't afford; while the land, if you didn't stop it from washing, would fill up the reservoirs and the navigation channel. But turn it around, move positively against this cycle of destruction, set up another cycle of restoration. . . .

Control the river and use the current to make fertilizer; that was the original TVA plan. But why not, also, stop erosion on the Valley farms because it increased flood hazards? Why not reforestation for the same reason? Why not tie the whole program together so closely that the Authority would have the support of persons uninterested in the controversial power policy?

This was not only the sensible thing to do, it was, when you studied the Act and the court decisions, mandatory. The legal plea for power was that it was incidental to the construction of a dam. The other activities of TVA were as clearly related to each other.

So began integration of the "multipurpose" program

which, explained in TVA literature and by every enthusiastic TVA employee, was to become not merely a legal explanation but a way of life for a region. Had there been no opposition to the power program, it is possible that TVA might have been chiefly a power project, building dams and selling electricity with no policy of Valley improvement beyond a faithful carrying out of the minimum provisions of the Act. But the need to make friends and allies in a struggle for existence taught the Authority to be a good neighbor, to extend its service in new directions and become firmly rooted in the life of the Valley.

The neatness and economy of the multipurpose idea appealed to Lilienthal's common sense, and its basic pattern of unity fitted into his philosophy. It afforded a perfect balance between his power program and Dr. H. A. Morgan's plans for farm improvement. Also it should, of course, have formed a perfect setting for the flood-control program which was the primary concern of Dr. Arthur Morgan.

The trouble was that Dr. Arthur Morgan didn't really take to the multipurpose idea, and it wasn't just because he hadn't thought of the thing himself. Actually, he seemed to dislike practical ways of dealing with the question of power; at times, certainly, he was not fully convinced that the Authority should sell power. His great work, before TVA, had been in the Miami conservancy district in Ohio, where construction was for flood control only and the dam bore a tablet forbidding any future power installation. In talking about public works Dr. Arthur Morgan was fond of using as an illustration the pyramids of Egypt, which were built to serve no useful purpose; but he neglected to mention Aswan dam, only half as useful as it should be because it was built to control Nile floods without harnessing power.

The chairman might have been more interested in power had he himself been able to deal with power sale, but he knew he was no businessman. As he once wrote, "Business ability is a power which has no necessary relation to a high type of intelligence and character." Not fully understanding business, it was easy for Dr. Arthur Morgan to distrust other people's conduct of it, and difficult for him to see that character could be displayed in business except as a rigidity of mind and a verbal "good faith," useless in dealing with corporations.

As an educator Dr. Arthur Morgan was interested in character building, and this interest carried over into his view of the whole TVA project. He felt that labor relations, for example, should be governed by considerations of personal character to a degree which to his associates seemed impractical and in fact undesirable. At about the time David Lilienthal announced the bill of rights for power, Dr. Arthur Morgan wrote out a code of ethics for TVA employees. The code was never officially promulgated for reasons which, to the other two directors, seemed adequate; those were the years when regimentation of public morals, instead of carrying the bracing atmosphere of New England, reminded people of a new European system being introduced by a man named Hitler.

The fact was that many of Dr. Arthur Morgan's recommendations for the Valley were good but impractical. He felt strongly, with Dr. H. A. Morgan, that the methods of farming should be improved; but he took the public stand that "laws of land ownership should be changed so that men shall not be allowed to own and occupy land unless they will manage it in the interest of a permanent agriculture." In this idea Dr. Arthur was only ahead of his time; the same argument was lately given government approval in England. But there it is directed against the land waste of big estates, while Dr. Arthur's criticism appeared to be aimed at the hard-up farmers who ploughed vertical corn rows in the Smokies. If he wanted to know how they would resist removal in the interest of a permanent agriculture, he had only to ask the TVA men engaged in reservoir clearance.

Another sound criticism of the South advanced by Dr. Arthur had to do with the county system, well known to be a useless survival from Manhattan to Mobile. In the South, if you consider the general poverty, it seems foolish for a county with fewer than four thousand people in it—there was one like that in the Valley—to support a complete set of officials with nothing to do but run the courthouse. On the other hand, you can say that with livings hard to make and salaries low, the county officials are permanently on WPA. The only thing wrong with Dr. Arthur's criticism was that TVA, coming in as a new regional agency, needed—for a time at least—the friendship of all the people it could get, even the county politicians and their relatives.

There were two ways of looking at the job of the Authority. One was that it would give you an opportunity to make over the Valley, and impose your own ideas or, as

Dr. Arthur Morgan would have put it, set a high standard for people to follow. The other view was that the Authority itself, the simple plan of fixing up the river and improving the soil and lighting the houses, would furnish a basis on which people could go to work to improve themselves. In that case you believed in the feasibility of the Authority so much that you worked only for its success, with the belief that other desirable things would follow in due time. Meanwhile, you felt you should be careful not to handicap the establishment of good relations for the Authority by introducing your own personal views of reform.

As far as Dr. Arthur Morgan's views were concerned, there was no question that they were not popular. Even audiences in little towns anxious for TVA power felt that Dr. Arthur's speeches were too much about a new social order, and not enough about Norris dam. On the other hand, newspapers in the Valley cities came right out and admired Mr. Lilienthal's friendly attitude, or his restraint, or his coolness under fire in the courtroom. Soon papers as far as New York and Washington began to quote his speeches and to mention that the youngest of the TVA directors was the man to watch. There was general approval except from the *Public Utilities Fortnightly,* which had long known the Lilienthal record in the field of cheap power, and which complained that less was heard of the "cottage industries" which had been the foundation of the TVA plan as first presented.

Lilienthal, whether or not the speech was intended to offset some of Dr. Arthur's criticisms of big industry, said in Chattanooga that "It is the Authority's duty as well as its privilege to encourage the growth of large-scale industry. This program should be based squarely upon the obvious benefits which industry will enjoy in the area."

As early as 1934, the Authority was attracting attention not only in other parts of the country, but in other countries. With Llewellyn Evans, the electrical engineer from Tacoma who became the TVA rates expert, Lilienthal went abroad in that year to see the new Shannon power development and to obtain firsthand information on the English "grid" plan for the pooling of power, which was highly praised as an example of co-operation between public and private enterprise. But as a subsequent power shortage was to prove, it was inadequate on the development side, and Lilienthal considered it no precedent for the Valley.

While he was in England Lilienthal made a BBC speech, in which he dealt prophetically with England's problem of decentralization of industry. It was TVA's problem, too, to reverse the trend to the cities in a region the size of England. And he made a political prophecy which has not lost its application:

To understand what is going on throughout America in these stirring times, there are two facts which you must have clearly in mind. First, you should know that President Roosevelt continues to hold the influence and the devotion of an overwhelming majority of American men and women from all classes and groups. And you should also realize that a powerful and reactionary opposition has begun a violent attack on his policy and on him. The outcome of this bitter controversy will determine the future course of American life.

The English trip had its usefulness for TVA; Lilienthal returned with the conviction that the power-grid plan was, for this country at least, a thing to be avoided. Dr. Arthur Morgan, on the other hand, admired it as the sort of friendly get-together with the utilities that he felt would be right. He prepared a power-pool plan which he continued to advocate and upon which he asked the advice of a former Insull engineer. Although the other TVA directors did not like the plan, the utilities, getting word of it, were as pleased by it as they always had been by the "no power" tablet on Dr. Arthur's Miami dam.

This difference was serious. It was awkward enough for the directors to disagree about minor matters, which could be adjusted; in some cases, as in the matter of building the town of Norris, Lilienthal and Dr. H. A. Morgan followed the chairman's proposals and, despite initial difficulties, came out all right. But it was impossible, with the utilities fight what it was, to have divisions on power policy.

Less serious in immediate consequence, but no less so in its implications for the future, was a difference about labor. Long afterward, Dr. Arthur Morgan was to claim that his views on labor had been misrepresented, and to say as well that these views had changed. So it is difficult, perhaps unfair, to say just what his views were beyond his own admission that at one time he had considered company unions, properly managed, a desirable solution. By his own later account he came to favor a friendly agreement with the crafts unions similar to one he had made on the Ohio project. For TVA, a labor policy was in fact worked out by Lilienthal and Gordon Clapp, present chairman of the

[ 39 ]

Authority, in collaboration with a craft-union expert; but TVA policy definitely did not exclude the new CIO unions which were just beginning in the Valley.

Whatever the Morgan views, Lilienthal's own ideas about labor were clear enough. In a Fourth of July speech at Chickamauga dam, the third big TVA dam to get under way, he said the trouble with many big enterprises was that management had "completely lost contact with the human beings who really make the machine go. . . . Human beings are different, thank God, from machines." And in a speech at Detroit, he admitted that in some cases, even in TVA, "discrimination because of union membership or activity" had been charged. In such cases, if the charge proved to be well founded, "then a change in supervisory staff took place." He thought TVA supervisors would "return to private industry with a new concept of the value of organized labor."

Somewhat later, not mentioning Dr. Arthur Morgan, David Lilienthal told an interviewer that if you knew a man's views on power and on labor, you ought to know where he stood otherwise. On both questions, it now appeared, there was a difference of opinion between the TVA chairman and the youngest director.

## III

## BRIDGES DENOUNCES
## "HITLERISM" IN TVA;
## INQUIRY IS DEBATED

ran a New York *Times* headline, March 10, 1938. Senator
S. Styles Bridges of New Hampshire had made a speech
in which he said "In the heart of America a new star has
arisen in the constellation of authoritarian states—the state
of Tennessee. And David Lilienthal is its Fuehrer."

This was funny on several counts, one obvious one being
that although people on the ground were willing to admit
that Tennessee was a dictatorship, everybody knew the
dictator was Boss Crump at Memphis. But Senator Bridges
was apt to make mistakes in identity. He said, for example,
that TVA had spent thousands of dollars for a jackass, to
improve the breed of draft animals in the Valley; the basis
for that statement was that construction engineers had
spent some hundreds for a mechanical jack.

Now, though, the Senator had a witness to speak for
him. Dr. Arthur Morgan, of all people, had accused Lilienthal of dictatorship and worse. For some time Dr. Arthur
had been taking his problems of conscience to the White
House and there accusing the other two directors of con-

spiracy against him. The President called everybody to Washington to talk things over, and only then did Dr. H. A. Morgan and David Lilienthal explain what troubles they had been having with Dr. Arthur.

Maybe it wasn't altogether news to the President, because Senator Norris had begun to suspect how things were going some time before. Of one of Dr. Arthur Morgan's well-meant pleas for getting together with the power companies, the Senator said, "I was amazed at Dr. Morgan's position. Had I read his statement without knowing its author I would have unhesitatingly declared that it was the work of a power trust attorney."

Norris continued, disposing of the complaints against Lilienthal, that the chairman "did not have a thing to prove his case. Dave had always consulted with me. I knew what he was doing, but I made a private investigation of my own, and found Morgan's charges to be false."

What Senator Norris knew about TVA, President Roosevelt knew. So when Dr. Arthur couldn't substantiate his charges against the other two directors but started lecturing the President instead, Roosevelt removed him from office for what he aptly called "contumacy." If Dr. Arthur had been smart he would have subsided right there while the whole country was looking up the word in the dictionary. But he didn't; he countered with making public accusations of dishonesty, no less, leveled against the other two directors. That really set up the headlines and Republicans from Maine to California started licking their chops with the hope that TVA would prove another, a Democratic, Teapot Dome.

[ 42 ]

Dr. Arthur Morgan didn't even agree that the President had the power to remove him from office. He spoke of the President's "endeavor" to remove him as if he might, as later he did, enter into a legal contest. Naturally he was at once a hero to all the anti-Roosevelt forces, and they panted with eagerness to hear what scandal he might disclose.

The thing to do was let him talk before the biggest possible sounding board. The great advantage in having Dr. Morgan state the case for the utilities was that he had a reputation for remarkable honesty. At the time he took the TVA job he filed with the Secretary of State an inventory of property possessed by himself and his family, and announced that he would submit a similar statement on leaving office. This looked like a beautiful innovation in public service, although it wasn't quite so practical as it seemed or even so unprecedented. David Lilienthal, undertaking the Public Service Commission job in Wisconsin, had make a report on his affairs to Governor La Follette; since then he had been continuously in public service at salaries set by law. Dr. H. A. Morgan was so well known to his Tennessee neighbors that he would have considered a statement of his assets a needlessly dramatic gesture. And of course a really dishonest person would find it easy to file a misleading statement. The TVA Act provided only that the directors should hold no stock in utilities or fertilizer companies. Actually, as the investigation was to show, Dr. Arthur had taken stock—in the sense of believing—in some utilities propaganda.

After his charges were printed, friends as well as enemies

[ 43 ]

of TVA were for an investigation to clear the air, but Senator Norris' proposal to let the Federal Trade Commission do the investigating was turned down. Instead, Congress voted for a joint inquiry by a House and Senate Committee, and Vice-President Garner and Speaker Bankhead duly appointed six Democrats and four Republicans to do the job. The committee then selected as its counsel Francis Biddle of Philadelphia, then known chiefly for his work with the old Labor Relations Board.

Hearings were to be held in the Valley all through that summer of 1938, but they began in Washington with a full turnout of flash bulbs. This was Dr. Arthur Morgan's day in court. He posed for the photographers, tall and commanding and photogenic in a snowy white suit with a tartan tie as crimson as a crusader's shield or an angry gobbler's wattles under his jutting jaw. The man he accused of attempting to dictate sat quietly among the other TVA lawyers. Except for a receding hairline, David Lilienthal still looked like an honor student.

Lilienthal listened gravely while Dr. Arthur, handled with silken courtesy by Mr. Biddle, first read a statement and then expanded on his startling premise that his fellow directors had been "dishonest." Years later, Lilienthal was to remark "That, even for as forgiving a cuss as I am, is a fighting word." But in his testimony, although he was given every opportunity, Dr. Arthur continued to utter only what Senator Norris called "glittering generalities," and on the whole he was a disappointment even to this eager audience. As a photographer muttered, gathering up

[ 44 ]

bulbs, he was a nice guy but he seemed to have missed a coupla fast ones.

When the committee moved to Knoxville the press went along, to spend warm weeks in the new Federal courtroom with its ceiling motto, "Let no man weakly conceive that just laws and true policy have any antipathy, for they are like the spirits and sinews, that one moves with the other." Reporters still hoped to find that scandal, but now the emphasis had changed.

Dr. H. A. Morgan, obviously unperturbed and even dryly amused, appeared for the first time to make a flat and uncompromising denial of the charges in which he, along with David Lilienthal, had been included. Dr. H. A. Morgan's position was peculiar; he was not so much defendant as witness and even judge, for he had long before taken his stand with David Lilienthal, and indeed the only complaint against him was that he had voted with Lilienthal. He appeared glad of an opportunity to affirm publicly policies he had already endorsed at board meetings. In fact, if anyone actually enjoyed the elaborate procedure of the investigation, it was Dr. H. A. Morgan, a quiet man who was to see the reasons for his own actions made dramatically clear.

Next to read a statement, David Lilienthal, looking somehow older and certainly responsible as he made his reply, allowed himself to show resentment of the charges. From the first day of Dr. Arthur's testimony it was obvious that in talking about "dishonesty" he had meant no peculation or maladministration of funds, but what he now called intellectual dishonesty, and illustrated by examples

[ 45 ]

which proved to be only disagreement with his own views. But Mr. Lilienthal refused to be mollified by a distinction between personal dishonesty and alleged official error. Years before he had told a meeting of the League of Women Voters in Chicago that public opinion should "make it just as heinous a civic offense to debauch the public business of light and power as it is to use trust funds for private gain." He insisted, now, on clearing himself from the mud of Dr. Arthur's charges if it meant going over every transaction made by TVA in its first five years.

As the Congressional committee was there to make a thorough investigation, with particular attention to TVA's power business, it looked like a long Southern summer. One of the Washington investigators, clambering over Hiwassee dam on a tour of inspection, had been heard to ask if North Carolina was a dry state. In the Knoxville courtroom they learned with regret that smoking was prohibited; as the testimony went on, one senator and one congressman resorted to chewing gum.

A succession of calm, solid engineers and office workers sat in the witness chair, embarrassing the investigators by familiarity with incomprehensible technical details. The Democratic committeemen were for the most part silent, letting TVA tell its own story, but the Republicans asked questions intended to be productive of pay dirt. The most aggressive examiner was Congressman Jenkins of Ohio; the most penetrating, Wolverton of New Jersey. Some members of the committee had campaigns for re-election to attend to back in their own states, but the Democrats timed their absences to coincide with TVA testimony while the Republicans stayed on the job hoping to catch a TVA witness out or to extract some really damning testimony from Dr. Arthur Morgan, who obviously didn't know what was legal evidence and what wasn't, but who certainly must know everything there was to know, and was anxious to tell.

One of his principal charges concerned the Berry marble case, a matter of claims brought by a former Tennessee senator for untold tons of unmined but presumably valuable marble drowned by Norris reservoir. The claimant was president of the Pressmen's Union and a person of political consequence in Tennessee, in fact a candidate for re-election that year. Because Senator Berry had acquired his land leases after hearing of government construction plans, it was obvious to Dr. Arthur that the Senator's claims were fraudulent, and he considered that only moral pusillanimity, or worse, moved his fellow directors to favor appealing for settlement to an appraiser borrowed from the Federal Bureau of Mines. The way to deal with a barefaced steal, said Dr. Arthur, was to call it a steal and have done with it. Mr. Lilienthal, on the contrary, had refused to call the claims fraudulent or to allow others to do so, out loud. Overlooking any need for legal caution, the former TVA chairman saw this as plain evidence of collusion with Berry. He never appeared to understand why this recital of shocking moral blindness on the part of the other two directors should fail to impress the senators and congressmen, or why they appeared, instead, sympathetically understanding of Mr. Lilienthal's testimony that the Berry marble claims had been handled ably, with complete integrity, and—slight pause—with gloves on.

Another matter about which Dr. Arthur felt strongly was the handling of land purchase, one of the minor administration problems entrusted to Mr. Lilienthal. This necessity for moving people off their farms had been a ticklish problem ever since Grandma Stooksbury had settled in her rocking chair, determined not to move until the rising waters of Norris reservoir should drown her out. Up North even the private power companies had trouble about moving farmers, and TVA had proceeded slowly, with care and caution and some expense. It was found that to the displaced farmers the question wasn't so much what they were paid as where they would move to; so the negotiations went on while TVA's relocation service undertook to find new farms. The hearings were remarkable for the absence of local complainants, but Dr. Arthur argued that in some cases the work of the land acquisition men had been too long drawn out. Let them fix a price, he said, a fair price, and have no oriental dickering.

A portly Republican congressman shifted his gum and leaned forward in his chair. "Then you would say, Dr. Morgan, that TVA paid too much for the land?"

At the press table the New York reporters stiffened, then relaxed as Dr. Morgan answered slowly, "Well, no, in some cases I'd say they paid too little."

"Too little?" The congressman was plainly unable to see how this could constitute maladministration.

"In some cases," Dr. Morgan conscientiously repeated

his qualification. So one by one the Morgan charges were disposed of, and the reporters began besieging Biddle with questions as to when Wendell Willkie would testify. Dr. Morgan had strong views about TVA rates—like Mr. Willkie and the Republican investigators, he thought them too low—but after the former chairman's general attitude had been made clear, the committee had no great hope of discrediting TVA's power policy through his testimony. He managed to convey his doubt of the wisdom of hiring an advertising agency to acquaint consumers with appliance use, although this highly successful campaign was one of the few things done by TVA which had the unqualified approval of the power companies. As for the TVA rates, Dr. Morgan's principal complaint was that Mr. Lilienthal had announced them without adequate consultation with the chairman. In view of other public power rates they might be all right; Dr. Arthur had once paid a visit to Tacoma, where the rate was lower, and had found everything in good order there, with—he said this with a significant yet slightly wistful emphasis—a beautifully disciplined staff.

As an engineer, Dr. Morgan also stressed his reluctance to see any use made of power from the dams except under very careful direction. Conscienceless people, he said, could endanger flood protection by thinking too much of power. This of course was true, but by this time the committee had come to have less interest in Dr. Morgan's conscience and more faith in the calm engineers who were still in charge.

What Dr. Arthur Morgan's whole testimony added up

to was his own belief in an exclusive right to righteousness. He knew he was a conscientious man; when other people disagreed with him they must be wrong morally as well as intellectually. More, he was chairman—a fact which, over and over, he emphasized. Chairman, and the only engineer among the directors of an engineering project. His voice never quite broke and he didn't burst into tears, as did one of the young TVA men, a former Antioch student with a deep sense of personal loyalty to the chairman, who was called to testify in his behalf. When Dr. Morgan's answers showed an excess of emotion Francis Biddle was quick to soothe him, and the questions went on.

There was emotion in the audience, too; TVA employees had to work, but their wives or other relatives attended the hearings, which furnished politically minded Knoxville with as much excitement as religiously inclined folk were finding in the Holiness revival being conducted at the same time. With shouts of "Come on, Holy Ghost, and fill this building!" the Holiness preacher attacked whisky, movies, rouge, and rolled stockings, and education—"I'd rather be in heaven reading the ABC's than in hell reading Greek." He accused the Communists of repealing prohibition and planning unemployment to create unrest. His hearers rolled on the floor.

A different sort of excitement filled the courtroom when David Lilienthal was called on to explain TVA rates. Here was material not only for the local papers but for the city men to cover. Four of the Democratic committeemen got away at this time, leaving Lilienthal to face a Republican majority, but heckling by Senator Frazier of North

Dakota did not shake his good humor nor force an admission that the rates fixed in 1933, before costs could be definitely determined, were only a lucky guess. Instead he took occasion to say that in his opinion TVA rates might be a little too high.

Returning reluctantly to the Morgan charges, the investigators had still to hear legal testimony answering the former chairman's complaint that he had not been given a chance to testify in court during various phases of the utilities suit which was still on its way to the Supreme Court. It was true that none of the directors had been called to testify, the lawyers in charge of the case agreeing that the constitutionality question could best be decided by other testimony. Nevertheless Dr. Arthur Morgan had wanted to have a say, had felt aggrieved because he hadn't been put on the stand, and the reasons governing this decision had to be explained by John Lord O'Brian, special TVA counsel in the suit brought by the power companies.

Mr. O'Brian explained that first of all Dr. Arthur Morgan in conversation with the lawyers had begun with a recital of grievances against his fellow directors, dating back to the beginning of TVA. Then he had asked whether, in establishing the constitutionality of TVA, it would be possible for the court "to declare part of the project to be constitutional and yet enjoin the rest of it." Mr. O'Brian had been discouraging on that point. "I told him that of course no one knows how a lawsuit would turn out, but I rather thought that if any such result was contemplated as that, the court would destroy the whole

[ 51 ]

thing, and declare it all to be unconstitutional. Once they got going on part of it, they might conceivably throw it all out. We came back to that subject several times."

Despite his own stanch Republicanism Mr. O'Brian was hopeful, he said, of "putting the conservation of water resources as related to electric power production on a constitutional basis, recognized by the courts." Dr. Arthur Morgan had said he thought that theory excellent, but he had other matters on his mind—the fact that he had been criticized by a newspaper columnist, the fact that he was not satisfied with the way TVA policies might be distorted by legal technicalities, and so on.

"Now, then," said Mr. O'Brian to his fellow lawyers on the committee, "if we had put the directors on the stand it would have been perfectly competent on cross examination to ask those directors about everything they had ever said or done about the TVA. . . . If Dr. Morgan had taken the stand he would have been cross examined." So, said Mr. O'Brian, he took the responsibility of saying that "under no circumstances would I agree to call Dr. Morgan as a witness." For, without questioning Dr. Morgan's accuracy or sincerity, the lawyer explained, "I have been conscious of the fact that he was greatly overwrought," that he was filled with resentment and certain to bring into the case on cross-examination views and irrelevant charges better kept out. "I think any lawyer would see that," said Mr. O'Brian, adding that otherwise the court case would have had brought into it "the same sort of thing I have been reading in the newspapers about your own hearing."

The committee understood only too well what Mr.

O'Brian meant. He spoke their language and they respected him. With his statement, serious consideration of Dr. Morgan's testimony was over—although ever since his explanation of the land claims it had been clear, to everybody but Dr. Arthur, that his accusations had fizzled out. His own view, stated to a friend as the hearing moved from Knoxville back to Washington, was that there was conspiracy in the investigation—Lilienthal and the committee counsel, that smooth-talking Francis Biddle, were in cahoots. Hadn't they gone to the same school, Harvard Law School?

The only hope now was that Wendell Willkie would be able to put up a real fight against Lilienthal. Mr. Willkie's health and his business commitments had time and again delayed his testimony, but in Washington he appeared, and cameramen had another field day as they focused on the genial, tousle-haired president of Commonwealth and Southern who had not, at that time, aspired to be President of the United States. He was at any stage of his career a picturesque figure, and people looked forward to verbal tilts with Francis Biddle, a different sort of lawyer. They were not disappointed, although you had to take a deep interest in electric power prices in order to understand what the gentlemen were saying.

The argument over TVA rates, which was more important to the investigators than any talk about management, had gone on long enough to produce great quantities of testimony on both sides. The utilities corporations brought in experts to tell what was wrong with TVA accounting, among them a Mr. Moreland who set forth in detail what should have been included in a sinking fund. His theme had been that charges for depreciation weren't set high enough, perhaps because utilities experience had been that dams sometimes leaked and reservoirs silted up, whereas nothing of the kind had happened or was expected to happen to the TVA installations. At any rate, depreciation charges were important to the whole rate question and it was considered relevant when Mr. Biddle led Mr. Willkie into a long discussion of depreciation as it affected rate fixing. Mr. Willkie was modest about it; he didn't, explained he, feel qualified to speak—he had more experts ready to testify if Mr. Biddle really wanted to know—but Mr. Biddle persisted. He just wanted to talk about the property of the Tennessee Electric Power Company, the depreciable property. The witness was a little reluctant to discuss this example because negotiations for sale of TEPCO to TVA were still going on; still, speaking only of depreciable property, let's say $90,000,000. . . .

That would be only depreciable property, said Mr. Biddle, so it would leave out land? Would Mr. Willkie call land depreciable property? No, Mr. Willkie would leave that out, as nondepreciable—

"I would leave it out too," said Mr. Biddle smoothly. "But Mr. Moreland didn't, and I was wondering. . . ."

This was the only opening that Mr. Willkie fell smack into, but the tiptoeing around and occasional sparring, with feints and parries, went on for several days with entertainment to the spectators and credit to both sides. After the hearings were over, Mr. Biddle was an obvious choice for the Justice Department and eventually for in-

[ 54 ]

vestigation of real dictatorship at Nuremberg, while Mr. Willkie was able to grapple successfully with a reluctant party convention.

The firecracker set off by Mr. Willkie in his testimony was his offer to sell the Commonwealth and Southern properties in the Valley to TVA for a price to be fixed by SEC. This looked like a beautiful idea and people outside the government thought it might be practical, but insiders said it was just a grandstand gesture to embarrass two government agencies, and SEC would refuse—as it did—to make the valuation. What the proposal really showed was that Mr. Willkie had reached the point where he would rather deal with any other agency than risk being outsmarted by Dave Lilienthal, in what Dr. Arthur would call "oriental dickering."

Lilienthal wasn't even on hand to hear Willkie's offer, having drunk unpasteurized milk and acquired a fever that took weeks in hospital to cure. At that he was up and about again before the Congressional committee, which took time out for November elections and spent the winter months digesting 15,470 pages of testimony from 101 witnesses, was able to issue the report which cost taxpayers nearly $75,000. In April, the committee said that Dr. Arthur Morgan's charges were "not well founded," specifically that "charges of dishonesty are without foundation, are not supported by the evidence; and, made without adequate consideration of the available facts, are unfair and unwarranted." The report explained that differences of opinion in the board of directors "became exaggerated out of all proportion because of the chairman's unfortunate propensity for attributing moral delinquencies to anyone who opposed him." It deplored "the tendency of the chairman to use words such as 'false, misleading and dishonest' when he means only that he disagrees." It added that "Dr. H. A. Morgan and Mr. Lilienthal, in the committee's opinion, acted with forbearance and dignity during the severe strain to which they were being subjected and with due consideration for proper administrative discretion. This cannot be said for Dr. A. E. Morgan." A minority report by three Republicans continued the objections to TVA rates but failed to uphold Dr. Arthur Morgan's charges, and the really remarkable thing was that one Republican senator signed the majority report upholding TVA on all counts.

Maybe the 15,470 pages of testimony were needed to make clear a fundamental fact about TVA as it appeared to David Lilienthal: the unity of the undertaking, a quality of wholeness in it which could resist every effort to break it up. Dr. Arthur Morgan's attitude was wrong not so much because the committee said it was as because the hearings disclosed his willingness to see nullified those parts of the program with which he himself had nothing to do—as Francis Biddle put it, to "seek a judicial decision against his own agency." There was a good Biblical parallel in the story of Solomon's decision to give the child to the woman who wouldn't have it cut in two.

A certain breadth of vision was required in order to see the project as a whole, just as a certain amount of imagination was needed to realize that low power rates would increase consumption sufficiently to justify the reduction, regardless of preliminary costs. At one time in the hearings Lilienthal let slip a doubt that Dr. Arthur Morgan ever had understood the low-rate premise, which was foreign to old-fashioned economics though familiar enough to a generation brought up on the price-cutting achievements of Woolworth and Ford.

The feasibility of low rates was in fact related to that idea of unity in multipurpose functioning which was the basis of Lilienthal's thinking; and it was this idea which Dr. Arthur, failing to grasp, unwittingly endangered. The investigating committee was amused when he stated uncompromising objection to the Pare Lorentz film "The River," to the making of which TVA had contributed, on the ground that the picture overstressed the importance of erosion as an element of flood control. The picture was, of course, made to explain the danger of erosion to people who had never considered the matter. Erosion was only one item in the far-reaching program of TVA; yet it did affect as apparently unrelated a problem as the price of electricity, since the silting up of reservoirs means loss at the powerhouse. But mainly, the big advantage of TVA lay in the fact that by curing the ills of the Valley—erosion and floods and abject poverty, lack of power—you made possible a health and strength that was out of all proportion to any fixed financial reckoning. You might as well try to measure by arithmetic the cost of getting a sick man well so he can go back to work; will he or won't he be able to earn enough to pay for the hospital care? Would it be better to effect only a partial cure, letting

[ 57 ]

him limp along for a while and not compete with his healthy neighbors?

In wanting to separate the various functions of TVA and save his own department—at one time in the testimony, Dr. Arthur Morgan made clear his candid opinion that only the hydraulic engineering, his contribution, was any good—Dr. Arthur more than justified the hopes of the power companies that he would do his best to help their case. Before the Congressional investigating committee made its report, he testified before the Rivers and Harbors Committee of the House in opposition to extension of the TVA plan of unified development. As his "secret" testimony was reported in the papers, the witness said people were taking water power too seriously; it would be better to go ahead with flood control and leave out power, and restrict any further regional authorities strictly to planning. He hedged about this thought with a good many conscientious and qualifying words; nevertheless, had he expressed it before his removal from the TVA chairmanship, it must have occasioned that removal. For under the Act, members of the board of directors were required to be "persons who profess a belief in the feasibility and wisdom of this Act."

Dr. Arthur Morgan and certain members of the investigating committee were not alone in their failure to see that the whole program of TVA, not any isolated part of it, constituted the true "yardstick." Much was made of a comparison of costs, as between private and public power, which could have only a limited validity. It might be instructive to learn, from a publicly announced breakdown of costs, that the private companies were overcharging in one particular; to this extent the rate comparison was useful, and TVA was bound to make its figures publicly known. But how in fairness could a separation of flood control and navigation charges, reforestation and erosion control and land use generally, be made for a government project as big as TVA? True economy lay in such a smooth blending of function as to make it a matter of opinion where one of the many purposes stopped and another began. The inescapable advantage of government as a provider of cheap power lay not in the fact that the government could operate more economically than the private corporation in the power field alone, but in the government's obligation to do other things capable of producing power. To separate these functions was in one sense as impossible as it was to dip up part of the river and say with certainty that this raindrop came from North Carolina, that mud from Virginia.

At the same time, as long as litigation challenged the right of the Authority to do this or to do that, the administrative necessity was to proceed by mutual consent, without disruptive argument, not as the individual spirit moved but as the letter of the law demanded. As the committee report said, David Lilienthal and Dr. H. A. Morgan acted with proper administrative discretion, a quality for which Lilienthal was to find continued and increasing use.

# IV

*Wherever water falls, power is created, and one of the express purposes of the TVA statute is that hydroelectric power so created shall be sold to assist in liquidating the cost of the project.*

> Decision of the U. S. District Court, Northern Division of Eastern Tennessee, in case of the Tennessee Electric Power Company *et al.* vs. the Tennessee Valley Authority.

IN A SPEECH at Memphis back in 1934, David Lilienthal had said, "The women will put TVA over." He had in mind, of course, the way farmers' wives were reaching for electric irons and washing machines and refrigerators and ranges. Judge Florence Allen of the Sixth Circuit Court of Appeals, who presided over the three-judge court at Chattanooga which heard the power companies' case against TVA in the winter of 1937, wasn't a housewife, but there was good reason to think she would decide for the Authority, as she did. In an earlier case, writing a minority opinion in a decision that went against federal housing, she had said, "The Government may undertake projects which benefit the health, the morals, and the general welfare of the people."

By the time the TVA case reached the appeals court, other judges had time to come around to Judge Allen's point of view, and the decision was unanimous. Although Wendell Willkie himself, not as lawyer but as witness, was there with forty other lawyers for the utilities, the court had its back to a wall on which a painting showed a web of power lines over farming country, the way only TVA had built them. That accomplished fact was bound to be in the judges' minds as they handed down a decision, in January, 1938, that said TVA had made its gains in fair and open competition and by honest contract.

The decision was a long one because it went into the "multiple-purpose" program of TVA, establishing—as weeks of testimony had shown—what the Authority actually had accomplished in the way of flood control and aid to navigation. The national-defense phase of TVA wasn't touched on beyond mention of a fact not then recognized as important, that a big chemical plant, the Monsanto works near Columbia, Tennessee, was a customer for TVA power.

But a Supreme Court decision would have to follow, and it was to take another year. The first test, carried to the Supreme Court in 1936, had dealt only with the disposal of surplus power from Wilson dam; in effect it had gone only as far as the dam-building program of World War I, and even then there had been a dissenting opinion from Justice McReynolds of Tennessee.

In 1939 Justice McReynolds still dissented, and had with him Justice Butler, but the majority opinion, read by Justice Roberts, was a complete justification of TVA.

[ 61 ]

Short but final, it was a disappointment only to some constitutional lawyers who hoped that the court would take the occasion to rule on due process. But the day the decision was handed down was dramatic enough, with a courtroom full of New Deal notables—Harry Hopkins, then Secretary of Commerce, Attorney General Frank Murphy, and others who had come not to hear the TVA decision but to welcome Justice Frankfurter to the bench. David Lilienthal was still too ill to be present, although he worked by telephone between bouts of fever.

Wall Street heard of the decision at lunch time but digestions were unimpaired; not even Commonwealth and Southern stock went down as much as a whole point. Recovered from its slight flurry, the market rightly paid more attention to a speech in the Reichstag being made that afternoon, by Chancellor Hitler.

In the Valley, the way was clear for buying out Wendell Willkie's companies, which could no longer hope for court backing. Mr. Willkie would, of course, have plenty to say about the price. With the Chattanooga court holding that the corporations had no recourse even if government competition should curtail or destroy their business, and countless utilities speeches to say that property would be worthless if the government continued to compete, it looked like a bad time to sell. But Mr. Willkie was a good trader.

Lilienthal, moreover, had no wish to see justified the utilities' claim that great damage had been done. Let Mr. Willkie talk of a "desperate situation"—the figures, Lilienthal pointed out as soon as he got out of the hospital, showed that

every one of his Southern companies did substantially more business last year than in 1933, when the TVA was created; every one of his companies had more net earnings last year than in 1933. The Tennessee Electric Power Company, in the very heart of the TVA area, increased its net earnings after charges for the twelve months ended November 30, in 1937, over the year 1936 by 13 per cent; these net earnings were 34 per cent greater than in 1933.

So you had the somewhat unusual spectacle of a prospective buyer declaring that the property under consideration was in good shape, while the seller complained that it was ruined. Despite these diverse views the two men understood each other very well.

Certain coincidences in background made fundamental differences in character stand out in bold relief. Both men were Indiana raised, and still recognizably Hoosier, although Lilienthal lacked the Middle West accent that remained with Willkie through life. Both were first-generation Americans, born of German-speaking parents who had come to the United States in search of better political and economic conditions, and had passed on to their sons a deep respect for the American way of life. But it was an interesting fact that the family background of the boy who grew up to be a corporation executive was Socialist. The Lilienthal family vote was progressive Republican, and in his school days the man who was to become head of a government agency attacked as "socialistic" wrote a little essay in favor of the presidential candidacy of Herbert Hoover.

From this you could argue that Lilienthal, administering a New Deal project, moved ahead of family training while Willkie was by temperament a conservative who moved back. Or you could attribute some of the difference to education; Lilienthal went to Harvard while Willkie got all his schooling in Indiana. But another interpretation, which subsequent behavior was to bear out, was that Willkie was slow in his own development. All he needed was more time.

Even at the time of the TVA contest Willkie, though older than Lilienthal, retained a boyish carelessness of manner which served as a perpetual excuse for the errors in power company statistics. Although federal investigation had disclosed the operation of a tremendous propaganda machine into which the corporations poured consumer money, TVA had to make its way through a jungle of new fabrications, each more ingenious than the last. The fact was that most people, though they hated paying bills, were confused by arguments about rates and didn't bother to figure out the difference between two mills and two cents a kilowatt-hour. But sometimes overelaboration spoiled the effect, and Wendell Willkie did better by sticking to the simple charge that TVA didn't pay taxes, a literal truth but a misleading statement in view of the amounts paid to cities and states "in lieu" of taxes. You couldn't stop Willkie from saying this even after President Roosevelt, speaking at Tupelo, had referred to the no-tax stories as "fairy tales." A soft-speaking Southern-born newspaperman tried it; given the customary publicity handout at Willkie headquarters he said, "Now, Mr. Willkie, I wouldn't say that if I were you."

"Why not?" asked Willkie.

"Because, Mr. Willkie, it just isn't so."

Willkie grinned, taking no offense, and took back the statement. But he didn't change the handout; it went on appearing in papers all over the country.

Willkie's grin and his bounce kept him going after heavier handed stuffed-shirt executives lost the battle. His trouble was that before TVA his companies lacked the enterprise to put on the low rates, the extension of service, and the drive for customers that, in the Valley, established TVA while raising the profits of private companies in the same area. Willkie led the utilities chorus that said there was already an excess of power in the Valley; in the early days the estimated overproduction was 30 to 50 per cent, and after TVA Mr. Willkie said it was 66⅔ per cent. David Lilienthal meanwhile kept on saying there would be a shortage, and he turned out to be right.

The unenterprising attitude of the corporations and the long campaign of complaint which they waged did work against them when it came to selling out. At the start, company propaganda had referred to a utilities investment of $500,000,000 in the Valley. Of course there was admittedly enough water in this big round figure to fill several reservoirs, and in the end bargaining between Willkie and Lilienthal got the purchase price down under $80,000,000. This, some people said, was $10,000,000 more than the stockholders expected to get. But back in the Wisconsin days Lilienthal had established a habit of considering the rights of investors, and, discounting the tears shed by Willkie for widowed and orphaned stockholders, he still did so. In a speech made at Brookings Institution just before he became a TVA director, he had pointed out some of the falsities in corporation claims but noted that it might not be in the public interest to demand "the last ounce of the constitutional pound of flesh" in dealing with the corporations.

American stockholders in TVA and consumers of Commonwealth and Southern power would have been interested in and perhaps edified by some of the conversations between David Lilienthal and Wendell Willkie which took place in Knoxville or New York or when the "two farm boys from Indiana," in Willkie's friendly but inaccurate phrase, took a walk around the Lincoln Memorial in Washington. Not that their political talk was important; during the Landon campaign, Willkie argued that Landon would win in a photo finish, with Ohio casting the deciding vote.

Smarter in his own field of business, Willkie could chuckle at the concern for his corporate interests expressed by the overconscientious first chairman of TVA. Whatever he said in public, Willkie knew from the balance sheet that his Southern companies were flourishing under TVA stimulus, as they continued to flourish after sale of the Valley territory to TVA.

From a business standpoint only, there can be no doubt that Mr. Willkie would have preferred to negotiate with Dr. Arthur Morgan. One of his persuasive articles in the

*Atlantic Monthly* had quoted the famous plaque on Dr. Morgan's Ohio job:

The Dams
of the Miami Conservancy District are for
Flood Prevention Purposes
Their use for power development
or for storage
would be a menace to
the cities below

Along with typical utilities publicity figures and such euphemisms as "capital costs" the article made an ethical appeal aimed straight at the man who was still TVA chairman, and Dr. Arthur Morgan was never deaf to ethical appeals. He had already heard and adopted such phrases of the Willkie vocabulary as "dismembered and destroyed." But there is reason to believe that Mr. Willkie would have been deaf, in the sense of being unimpressed by radical social arguments that might have been advanced by Dr. Morgan. His mind would have been on getting the chairman to sign on the dotted line.

Business aside, Willkie and Lilienthal were observed to be on friendly terms and the president of Commonwealth and Southern was said to be curious about a man willing to work as hard as Lilienthal was working for $10,000 a year, when any utilities corporation would have paid him enough to make that look like peanuts. In the process of discovering what made his opponent tick, Willkie would have found out, probably, more about the world outside his own experience than he found out about the man;

Lilienthal is not a man to talk about himself. But he will talk at the drop of a hat about the duties of a public servant, or grassroots democracy, or power developments in foreign parts; he is also eloquent on the principle of unity, in a river system or in the world.

Wendell Willkie liked talking too, and there was more common ground to start with than some people would have believed. But it was found by Willkie on Lilienthal's side, not the other way round. Regarding utilities regulation, for example, Willkie conceded in a speech made in New York in 1938 that "our industrial activities and our social needs have outgrown regulation by states alone."

When at the conclusion of negotiations Willkie pocketed a TVA check it looked like the end of a business deal in which both sides had done well enough, and the contest was ended. For TVA it was. But Wendell Willkie was a long-term fighter, and it may be that he took away, besides the purchase price of Commonwealth and Southern holdings in the Valley, a determination to find out what there was in this public-service game. Soon after, he made a good try to get into it as he had gone into the power business, at the top.

Later, he had a look at the prospects for unity all over the world. On the trip he saw with surprise—and "I am not one to be easily surprised by vast governmental power developments"—a dam-building project on the Volga which, completed, "would produce twice as much power as all the TVA, the Grand Coulee, and the Bonneville developments combined." A reader of *One World* submitted to Mr. Willkie several questions suggested by this passage:

[ 68 ]

Do you agree that development of large power projects, from the Arkansas to the Danube, would be a useful postwar activity?

Do you believe that this development should be left to privately owned corporations?

If left to private enterprise, do you see any way to make power dams serve also for flood control, in interrelated regional systems?

If left to private enterprise, do you believe that power development in the United States after the war can be counted on to proceed as rapidly as, say, the rebuilding of the Dnieperstroy dam in the Soviet Union?

Mr. Willkie was still a utilities executive and not a public servant; instead of answering the questions, he wrote:

"I do wish I could answer them, but the pressures on me are almost unbelievable, and it is just impossible for me to find the time to really develop my attitude on this subject."

It is just possible that this reply, cagey as it seemed, was the simple truth. Although Willkie was slow in starting to think about the world, in the short time he gave to the subject he made rapid progress. He was not too old or too stuffy minded "to really develop." But the time was shorter than he knew.

Conclusion of the Commonwealth and Southern negotiations brought general satisfaction, to TVA, to the stockholders, and to the editorial writers. The Authority promptly announced a series of conferences with state and local agencies to discuss an increase in the percentage of power revenues to be paid "in lieu" of taxes, versus an increase in the share returned to the Federal taxpayers. Five years later, Governor Arnall of Georgia was to say "I believe the states actually have received more money under the TVA system of payments in lieu of taxes," and to go farther: "I might add that privately owned utilities have benefited from the advent of TVA, having been stimulated to render more service, with the result that their profits increased."

There was only one loser. The day the deal was decided in the Lilienthal kitchen at Norris, Mrs. Lilienthal had made a batch of chocolate cookies for David, Jr., to take on a camping trip. When the eighty-million-dollar argument was over, the experts for TVA and for Commonwealth and Southern, filling the house and using the kitchen telephone, had gobbled up every cooky.

## V

*Once an old man in the North Georgia hills, who was quite mad and had fought at Chancellorsville and claimed to be of the Appins, told me that, come Armageddon, they will play "Dixie" on the pipes.*

ELLIS GIBBS ARNALL, *The Shore Dimly Seen*

A SMALL GROCERY STORE in Knoxville boasts  sign that reads "Owned and operated by East Tennesseans." To be one kind of Southerner, you have to be as local minded as that. Even after he'd been years in the Valley, David Lilienthal couldn't hope to be that way.

But there is, and has been since Jefferson's day, a kind of Southerner who holds to the South after having had the opportunity to compare it with other places. Up in Philadelphia or over in England or France, Jefferson was always seeing useful inventions—not political or social inventions, but practical scientific ones—that he wanted to try out at home, where he knew the natural advantages were the best in the world. Your true Jeffersonian wants to live in the South and to use there, as is right, a few useful Yankee gadgets.

Bringing down the best set of tools ever offered to Americans anywhere, Lilienthal could be that kind of

Southerner, and as soon as TVA got a clear legal title he settled down to the job. Administrative purposes did not change, but policies did, much as in Roosevelt's day many of the objectives of Woodrow Wilson were attained by opposite methods. There was no overturning of people on jobs after Dr. Arthur Morgan left and Dr. H. A. Morgan succeeded him as chairman; a few people who felt a personal loyalty to the first chairman chose to leave, but nobody was fired. Senator Pope of Idaho became the third member of the board, and after four more years Lilienthal took over the chairmanship. By that time, bygone differences had become the basis for stories like the one about Lilienthal and the ham. In Kentucky, the story goes, a farmer offered a fine home-cured ham as a present and shook his head when the Lilienthal policy of taking no presents was explained. "What's the matter with you TVA men? Fellow came through here a while back and I offered him a ham and he wouldn't take it either. Name of A. E. Morgan. I said then, a man that didn't have sense enough to take a Kentucky ham didn't have sense enough to build a dam." Lilienthal reconsidered and took home the ham.

Although no TVA chairman would try to set up as a planter or a political lawyer, two time-honored Southern occupations, the TVA farm program was a mighty big plantation and there was always plenty of legal business for TVA. If there was no big plantation house, the architecture of the dams and of the towns built around them was good enough to occasion an exhibit at New York's Museum of Modern Art.

After construction ended at Norris and houses were

available, the Lilienthal family—including a cocker spaniel the color of copper wire—had moved to a white cottage at 81 Pine Road. As the years went by, Lilienthal kept right on living in the little Norris house. He'd made a rock garden there, and leveled a badminton court out of the hill in back. In time the rock garden would become a Victory garden, and by that time, had the war been one between the states, Lilienthal's neighbors would have expected him to be on their side.

Never a man to put on airs, the only thing he did that was a plain throwback to Jefferson's day was ride a horse around Norris. The horse was a big bay named Mac, said in his prime to be a five-gaited or multipurpose animal; eventually he got so gentle that Lilienthal let the Norris children have free rides on his back. Maybe there is some sort of symbolic meaning in the Lilienthal fondness for horses, or horsepower; besides Mac, Lilienthal acquired a collection of smaller inanimate horses made of pottery or metal which still takes up shelf space in his study. The collection started with family Christmas presents, related in some way to a joke about "Git a horse," but there is an Indian pottery specimen which Lilienthal fell in love with and bought for himself down in Mexico, and which, Mrs. Lilienthal says, was harder than a live horse to carry home. This Mexican horse has a Tasco Indian on his back, and it could be that Lilienthal likes the reversal of the historical man-on-horseback conquest.

The year 1938, besides clearing up misunderstandings about TVA, brought a clear survey of things needed to be done in TVA territory. The National Emergency Council, directed by Lowell Mellett, brought in its famous report that pointed to the South as the nation's "Number One Economic Problem." The report told the things that well-informed Southerners already knew, and stressed one point that for years had marked the difference between a Southerner and a Yankee. That point was freight rates.

David Lilienthal hadn't waited until 1938 to know about that. Back in 1934, in a speech at Birmingham, he had proved himself already a good Southerner by expressing his sympathetic understanding of that problem. For Northern readers who still don't know, it should be explained that for years the Northern-owned railroads made as big a difference between Southern shippers and Northern shippers of freight as Southern prejudices made between white and colored passengers. The Jim Crow freight rate was higher, so much higher that it kept the South a hard-up farm country by penalizing industry. Southern oratory had long held forth on the freight differential, which could be considered partly responsible for the wage differential and the school differential and all the other differentials that made the South a conquered province. But when it came to changing rates, the South just didn't have the votes.

At Birmingham Lilienthal promised that TVA would make a survey that might help move Yankee minds by putting the thing plainly, in dollars and cents, and TVA did do that. Even more important to Southerners who were cynical about Yankee help, he talked in a way that sounded as if he really might make a good Southerner. As the Birmingham *News* put it, "Mr. Lilienthal was frank; he exhibited understanding, and quite notably, moreover, he identified himself and TVA with the people of this section of the country. He would speak, for example, of 'our' problems, of factors which have operated 'against us,' of enterprises for 'our' benefit, and of how, with reference to the South's unfavorable trade balance, 'we' buy more than 'we' sell. His use of those pronouns is to be appreciated. Mr. Lilienthal comes from Wisconsin, but he is obviously now a citizen of the region, not only in official capacity, but in sympathies and interests as well."

Besides making a freight-rate survey, TVA offered competition with the railroads—a freight yardstick—in the movement of freight along the river, as soon as the dams could make a navigation channel. It was the freight-rate situation that made Tennessee shipping more important than any visitor, looking at the sleepy river, could understand. When TVA moved its own construction housing by water from Pickwick dam to Gilbertsville, it was a sight not only startling but significant.

Lilienthal not only learned Southern farm language, so as to talk about cottonseed and soybean processing without sounding like a Yankee smarty; he found things to say which hadn't been said before. Southerners are only too familiar with political sweet talk about the magnificent resources of their country; what they want to know is why, with all those resources, they have no money to spend. Lilienthal could summarize the usual speech in a sentence: "Almighty God has been generous with the South." But he went on from there, as for instance to a farm group in Georgia back in 1938, to explain how the gifts of the

[ 75 ]

Almighty were being drained away and—most important—
how some of them might be got back. To the Georgia
audience, which included 4-H boys and girls and their
families, he admitted that the most serious loss was the
loss of good people—"many of our best trained young men
and women are drained away from us." But he suggested
that things were changing, that people in the South were
waking up to their advantages and, conversely, it could be
seen that difficulties were general. "It is becoming more
and more apparent to all of us that the economic problem
of the farmer and of the worker in the cities and of the
business man is a problem common to all groups. That
problem is how to increase the nation's income; and then,
having increased that income, how to insure the permanence of democratic institutions by seeing to it that the
income is fairly and equitably distributed."

As a practical example he went on to tell what had happened on a farm down in Mississippi, where a farmer with
nine children—seven boys and two girls—had been having
a harder time than usual because of a fire that ruined his
place, followed by a breakdown in health that put the
responsibility of the farm on the two oldest boys, fourteen
and sixteen. These boys were good 4-H members, winning
prizes for hogs, corn, and cotton, and keeping things going
for a while on their prize money. Then they got TVA electricity, wired the house themselves and gave their mother
a radio for Christmas. In time the two oldest boys went
off to college, leaving the others to carry on because work
was lighter after the farm was electrified. You saw from
this story what was being said all over the Valley, that with

farm conditions improved by electric power, boys would leave only to get more education—then they'd go back.

Besides keeping the human resources, Lilienthal was interested in finding ways to use and earn from the mineral resources and the crops and timber which, sent out of the South as raw materials, brought an inadequate return. This is a problem of the Middle West and the Southwest as well as of the old South, and he used a common interest in TVA phosphates to tie in what should be a common interest in raising processing profits. Talking to a group of newspaper publishers at Mineral Wells, Texas, in 1940, he started with the difference between what a farmer would get for a load of pulpwood and what the same wood would bring processed first into pulp and then into paper. He carried the comparisons through with cotton made into yarn and cloth and shirts, and with asphalt into roofing, and with aluminum ore into kitchenware. He blamed the industrial lag on the freight rates, as Southerners were accustomed to do, but he mentioned another factor: industrial research, to develop new processes and adapt them to local conditions. He admitted that most of the research was being done by big corporations in the North and East, but he gave credit to new southern developments—a paper industry in Texas that owed its existence to the Herty experiments with Southern pine at Savannah, Georgia, and a promise of industrial research at the University of Texas. He told something of what was being done at the University of Tennessee, in co-operation with TVA. And he said what his hearers knew, and the country needed to know, that "The kind of country we shall be twenty-five

[ 77 ]

years hence will depend largely upon what happens in the South in the coming years."

These prewar discussions were important in view of the wartime expansion of Southern industry that was to come. The war would settle the question of Southern industrialization, but it was important to think of it in time to try to avoid some of the troubles that quick and careless industrial growth can bring. Many hard-up Southerners were so hungry for factories that they would take them on any terms—no taxes, slave wages—trusting the whole welfare of a town or a state to the mercy of a manufacturer. Lilienthal was more cautious and conservative. Speaking to a wartime audience in Virginia in 1944, he said:

We in the South are going to have industry, almost whether we like it or not. But we need not—and this is the theme of my remarks—have an industrialization that brings with it all the evils of congestion, ugliness, absurdly large cities, uncomfortable living, and consequent social strains. We do not need to choose between pastoral poverty and industrial hideousness. . . .

If we are wise, if we are intelligent and farsighted, if we conscientiously use the tools at hand, history may be able to record this heartening result: the Southeast was able to industrialize and yet avoid the penalties that other regions of the country and the world have paid.

Among the safeguards Lilienthal listed cheap electricity, a clean and mobile power—"the greatest single decentralizing force of modern time," giving small communities and individual households city comforts in rural peace. He cited the fact that although income in the Tennessee Valley, not counting the war boom, had risen more rapidly than over the country as a whole, the movement of population to the big cities was less in the Valley than elsewhere in the South.

But first and most important he mentioned, ahead of electricity, local and regional planning by the people themselves. He reminded the Virginians that this was no new idea—under early Anglo-Saxon law, a man had to get the permission of his community in order to build a slaughterhouse or set up any other activity that could be called a nuisance. He didn't suggest that some of the new war industry was of that description; he was to make other speeches, at Chattanooga and elsewhere, about the practical problems of converting war plants to useful purposes. Now he was talking about regional planning, and he stressed the idea that there was no irreconcilable difference, necessitating an all-out choice, between agriculture and industry. By realizing the unity of natural resources and their utilization the South could develop as a whole, combining productive land use with the processing of local products. As an example of basic adjustment he cited "one of the greatest of all factory processes—the dairy cow."

The unity argument—land and river, agriculture and industry, the South and the rest of the country—comes up over and over again in Lilienthal's thinking, and while he came to think like a Southerner you could never say that he stopped thinking like a citizen of the rest of the country and of the world. It was only that, there in Tennessee where the physical division had been, he insisted on taking the South back into the Union. To do that he had first of all to understand and sympathize with local Southern attitudes.

The freight-rate problem, being a thing known to everybody in the South but curiously hard to explain up in New York, or Chicago, or Washington, offers an excellent illustration of why TVA became famous as an agency of decentralization. There are problems that are plain in Tennessee or Alabama that, with the best will in the world, you can't see in the political power center of the nation. As he got to be a good Southerner David Lilienthal understood this better and better, and in his later years in the Valley he came to preach regional and local autonomy in terms that warmed the heart of every grassroots listener. Not States' rights—that argument had been taken over by the politicians up in New England who didn't like federal projects. Lilienthal could if necessary prove that TVA did no harm to the states, and as TVA spread its benefits the state governors in the Valley were always ready to prove it for him. But he was concerned for areas smaller than states; he wanted the farmers of Alcorn and Wheat communities to have a say-so about their own affairs, and the storekeepers at Decatur, and the hard-up people in a little hill place called Happy Hollow. So TVA started at the bottom and worked up exactly the way Jefferson, in writing about how he'd like to organize the country, wanted to start with the school ward.

This made Lilienthal, speaking politically, a very rugged individualist; and the president of a big corporation, testifying before a Congressional committee, was so to describe him. Mr. Chester I. Barnard of the New Jersey Bell Telephone Company said, "I concluded from my association with him that Mr. Lilienthal was about the greatest individualist that I have ever met." In private discussion, Mr. Barnard went on to say, Mr. Lilienthal had "evinced a stronger fear and a more deep dislike of the centralized bureaucracy of the federal government than any man I have ever met in business or out of business."

Lilienthal said it for himself in his last speech as TVA chairman, made in Philadelphia before the National Municipal League. He talked against "big government" as definitely as some reformers talk against big corporations, and he used the Valley, naturally, as his example:

The TVA has by persistent effort delegated and thereby decentralized its functions so that most of them are carried out not by federal employees at all, but by local and state personnel. This is effected by scores of contrasts setting up joint partnership between TVA and cities, towns, counties, state boards of health, state conservation commissions, city power boards, *farmers,* co-operatives, county extension services, state agricultural colleges, state geology departments—I could continue this list almost indefinitely.

A queer thing was that as it became known as a grassroots project, concerned with freezing local strawberries and testing the taste of sorghum ice cream, and discouraging mosquitoes while increasing the number of fish in the river, TVA began to attract the envious attention of other regions all over the country. At the start President Roose-

[ 81 ]

velt had seen clearly the division of the country into several, perhaps seven, power regions; but this New Deal planning was not at first appreciated by the regions themselves. It took the example of TVA to start a demand for other Authorities coming as it had to come, from the grassroots.

Of course a genuine grassroots demand grows more slowly than a centralized government moves, so TVA remains the only authority of its kind in the country; but ever since 1934, when the first bills to authorize an Arkansas Valley Authority and a Missouri Valley Authority were introduced in Congress, plans have been drawn for such regional developments. They'll come in time. For the planning, hopeful people from Arkansas to Oregon turned to TVA, and David Lilienthal was asked for advice about the many problems involved. True to his individualist philosophy, he has insisted that the various regions consider their own separate needs, using TVA as an example but not a model to be copied in detail—you can't turn out more Valleys "with a cooky-cutter."

What you can see, and what flood damage will perhaps make clear, is that the country isn't getting the fullest good out of TVA flood control as long as one Authority works alone. It's as if you had Norris dam but not Hiwassee and Fontana and the other twenty-odd that, by working together, control the river. The Tennessee is under control but the Tennessee is only a branch of the Ohio, which is a branch of the Mississippi. It will take a Missouri Valley Authority and a few more to make Old Man River roll smoothly, and so get a full return from the TVA investment. Maybe more floods and a depression as well, with a public works program, will come first.

Some say that there would have been an Arkansas Valley Authority or a Columbia Valley Authority by now if it hadn't been for the war, and some say if it hadn't been for Harold Ickes. Honest and sensible about most things as everybody knows he is, the curmudgeon of the Interior Department wouldn't call himself tactful, and so he couldn't be expected to see the advantages of the regional plan—advantages which have to do with considering local views and soothing local fears. When more Authorities were talked about, Roosevelt was always for them but Mr. Ickes was always against them unless they could be co-ordinated, from the start, under Department of Interior administration. Of course the whole advantage of the regional plan is to escape such a close federal tie-up, and allay the apprehensions of proud people all over the country who don't want to be beholden to Washington. It was natural for Mr. Ickes, who had done such a good job with his department, to feel that regional Authorities would gain rather than lose from the association. It was true that under stress of war, for example, it would be necessary for the regions to act together under federal control. But as a matter of practical politics, or tact, Mr. Ickes should have let the regional plans get started and firmly under way before talking of co-ordination.

Otherwise you had the sort of administration from the top down that Dr. Arthur Morgan had once advocated for the Tennessee Valley. An odd thing was that just as Dr. Arthur Morgan had once decided that David Lilienthal was a dictator because he stood out against that sort of dictatorship, Mr. Ickes jumped to the conclusion that Mr. Lilienthal was personally ambitious when he held out for regional planning against Mr. Ickes' departmental control. So when the Atomic Energy Commission appointment came through Mr. Ickes was one of the few newspaper columnists who failed to applaud it, and to know why you had to know the history of that whole regional versus Interior Department argument. Few people knew because, as in the early days at TVA, administrative differences of opinion were not publicly aired. But as impartial testimony you could take the view of a man whose job gave him a chance to see the dispute at close range, without impelling him to decide one way or the other—a man in the position of Dr. H. A. Morgan. This time the man was "Cap" Krug, former power manager for TVA, later Secretary Ickes' successor in the Interior Department. It was not as a TVA employee but as Secretary that Mr. Krug spoke out for a Columbia Valley Authority on the TVA plan, not under his own direction from Washington.

Or you could listen to a scientific opinion. That the region is about as far as the average citizen's patriotism will stretch was pointed out by a qualified observer of the human mind, the anthropologist Dr. Margaret Mead, who told a Texas audience that Americans might as well learn to solve their problems on a regional basis because they never seemed to get together on a national level.

More important, you could listen to the people in the regions where it was proposed to develop new flood control, power, and—in the West—irrigation projects. These people themselves listened with interest when David Lilienthal said that TVA had "responsibility to see that things happen—but no powers of compulsion." They were happy to hear him say that TVA had no power and wanted no power to order around farmers, businessmen, local or state governments, or citizens generally. They applauded out in St. Louis when he told them over the radio that "In the Tennessee Valley a large chunk of the federal government has been taken right out of Washington and rooted in that Valley." So rooted, the country might come to feel for the federal government an affection which so far, broadly speaking, it has never felt.

You could put it another way and say that by setting up a system of publicly owned power, managed from the grassroots, the Valley was emancipated from the dominion of corporations centered in another part of the country. When Knoxville bought out the local power plant, shareholders met and approved the deal up in Augusta, Maine. When the check was handed to Commonwealth and Southern, it was in the office of the First National Bank in New York.

To get back to Lilienthal's living in the Valley and learning how to be a Southerner, a good sign of how well he came to feel at home there, and how Southerners take him for one of themselves, came when they had a ceremonial dedication of Kentucky dam. You have to remember that although Kentucky is the state that has a TVA dam named for it, Kentucky uses little TVA power; by an old law, Kentucky cities were prohibited from constructing the municipal power plants which distribute TVA power.

[ 85 ]

Kentucky newspapers such as the Louisville *Courier-Journal* could be enthusiastic about TVA, as they were, but the state just couldn't ask for an allotment of TVA electricity which, in the opinion of some people like Congressman May, might compete with Kentucky coal.

Of course they were glad to have the dams built, and the Paducah Chamber of Commerce had a dinner to celebrate, with President Truman down to speak, and a torrential flow of Southern oratory besides. It was pretty late when they called on David Lilienthal, and everybody had said about everything that could be said in praise of Kentucky, and TVA, and the new dam, several times over. So Lilienthal got up and grinned and said only, "I'm very sorry, gentlemen, that as far as I can see, Kentucky stands no chance whatever to get any of the power from this dam."

Down South, when you feel you can come out with flat deflationary truths of that kind, and they let you get away with it and chortle over it afterward the way they do, you can know that you are one of the family. It's not true that you can't achieve the honor of being a Southerner if you really work at it; Dr. H. A. Morgan, though most people consider him a Tennessean, was born in Canada. So David Lilienthal had an inspiring example of successful adaptation always before him.

It's not true either that the South, given time and other things to think about, can't bury the Civil War. Time has helped, and the rapid turnover of the generations in a region that marries young. Instead of grandfathers who wore the gray you now hear them say, down South, "You see, his grandfather was killed in the first World War, so when he went up North in this war—" That has made a difference. But of course the biggest help of all has been TVA, really reconstructing—or helping the Southerners to rebuild for themselves—that country from Knoxville to Shiloh where the fighting was worst.

There has been a conscious effort to tie TVA in with history; the first dam built after Norris was named for a Confederate general, and when they dedicated Chickamauga dam back in 1938 they invited President Roosevelt down to ceremonies that would commemorate the seventy-fifth anniversary of the battles of Chattanooga, Chickamauga, Lookout Mountain, and Missionary Ridge. The Tennessee delegation told the President that this would give people over the country a chance to see the great effort being made "to rehabilitate and conserve the natural resources and the human values that are a potential part of the Tennessee Valley," though "grievously injured by the mistakes of the past." They said that the great undertaking of the Tennessee Valley Authority "must forge its way to ultimate success against the opposition of the greed of unwarranted and unjust privilege on the one hand and the ignorance of unwarranted and unjust poverty on the other," and that under the helpful guidance of this great agency of government, the ingenuity of man was "harnessing the dark forces of a river of death" to make a river of life.

The celebration of Chickamauga scheduled for September, 1938, had to be postponed to November because the

President had other matters, among them a meeting at Munich, on his mind.

Of the people at Chickamauga, at least one other man was bound to be thinking of Munich too, for there they were disposing of a "small, faraway country" which had been the home of David Lilienthal's father before he came to the United States. Leo Lilienthal had never gone back, and his son had made only the one trip abroad, to England. When they talked of going back together to see modern Czechoslovakia, where there were interesting developments in hydroelectric power, the elder Lilienthal said, "You go if you want to—I had all of Europe I wanted. I came here to stay, and I never intend to go back."

As they had fought one war along the Tennessee to make the South a part of the country, men were to fight another war to make the country and all countries part of the world. In Knoxville, during that war, knitting-mill pickets appeared dressed in sheets and carrying placards that read "Mahatma Gandhi wins with non-violence—so will we." Returning the global compliment, at New Delhi this year a speaker for the proposed Damodar Valley Corporation explained how the plan represented the application in public affairs of the best practices of modern business management, providing for "maximum flexibility" and "multipurpose development"—in short, for a TVA in the Indian states of Bihar and Bengal.

Wherever he might live, David Lilienthal was bound to be a citizen of the world, but he was firmly rooted by the Tennessee River. His son David would go to the university at Chapel Hill, as his young brother Allen had gone to medical school at Memphis and married a Memphis girl. When he got time he himself intended, as literate Southerners always intend, to write a book. But he kept his mind, as a good Southerner should, on the problems of the Southern farmer. Speaking in 1937 in Virginia, he said, "Of course the Act that created the TVA does not say in so many words that the Authority is directed to bring about an increase in the income of farmers. But that is one consequence of the Authority's program, if the directions of Congress are successfully carried out."

There are figures to show that the program was carried out, but one little fact will prove it as well. In 1946, the *Progressive Farmer* named David Lilienthal the "man of the year in Southern agriculture."

# VI

MAGNUS: *When all the frontiers are down London may be outvoted by Tennessee, and all the other places where we still madly teach our children the mentality of an eighteenth century village school.*

LYSISTRATA: *Never fear, sir. It is not the most ignorant national crowd that will come out on top, but the best power station; for you cant do without power stations, and you cant run them on patriotic songs and hatred of the foreigner, and guff and bugaboo, though you can run nationalism on nothing else.*

BERNARD SHAW, *The Apple Cart*

ONE of the truest prophecies ever made by David Lilienthal was that for TVA there would "never be a time when we can settle back and say that the hard and hazardous part of the job is done, that the rest is day-to-day administration." For he said this in 1939.

National defense was the least popular of TVA's multiple purposes; good TVA men didn't even like to remember that the old Muscle Shoals plant was built to make explosives. They were all for better plowshares, not swords, and nobody wanted to see the Valley become what everybody knew it could be, the Ruhr of America.

But David Lilienthal never forgot the national-defense

specification of the act, and every year when he went to talk to Congress he mentioned it. In 1935, being one of the people who never did like Hitler, he referred to Nazi conscription in answering the perennial question about overproduction of power. Mr. May's Military Affairs Committee still worried about a possible surplus, but Lilienthal waved at them a copy of the morning paper with the news of Nazi war preparations. Even the TVA staff members who had gone along were afraid at that time that Lilienthal along with Roosevelt would be called a warmonger.

When in due time the Germans invaded Poland, Lilienthal gave the President a memorandum saying exactly what TVA was prepared to do in case of war. Another memorandum went to the White House at the time France fell.

Back in 1938 and 1939, while headline writers hailed peace between the power companies and TVA, and between the holding companies and SEC, President Roosevelt and the War Department started checking and discovered, as the President wrote to an emergency committee, "a shortage of power to meet the needs of the nation's industry in the event of war." But the private utilities were in no hurry to provide additional power capacity. "Utilities to Spend Little More in '39," said a New York *Times* headline, adding "TVA Peace Not Enough—Greater Assurances Desired Before release of Funds for Capital Outlays."

Then it was that the government began planning in earnest to make the Tennessee Valley the production center of the country that was beginning to call itself the arsenal of democracy. The old Muscle Shoals factories were rebuilt and reconditioned: there were new appropriations for power to step up the manufacture of aluminum for war planes.

Congress didn't move so quickly, but it did authorize Cherokee dam while TVA put Watts Bar to work eight months ahead of schedule. Then began a struggle over additional construction; the House Appropriations Committee held up funds for Douglas dam until William L. Batt of WPB made a public protest. The Douglas project was one that a pressure group of Tennesseans didn't want, because its reservoir would drown out some good farmland and necessitate moving some canning plants. Senator McKellar in particular was opposed to the dam, and, as always, the senior senator from Tennessee had considerable influence on his Congressional colleagues. However, Mr. Batt warned of a serious power shortage in 1943 if the dam wasn't built, and his speech was effective—perhaps because he made it December 4, 1941, three days before Pearl Harbor.

In May of that year David Lilienthal proposed that the Authority triple its power production, to make "a pool of over fifteen billion kilowatt-hours of electricity each year, the largest single pool of available energy ever created in the history of mankind." To do it would take ten new dams, but these could be built in record time. Lilienthal warned that "We will have shortages of aluminum and steel and magnesium and other basic commodities as long as we have a shortage of courage to put American resources to work."

This time they really did get started on the new dams, and from then on TVA piled up a war record that was hard to believe. Before 1941 was over, the Cherokee dam was done, to set an all-time construction record.

By 1942 the Authority had a new employment record—42,000 people were building six new dams, installing new power equipment, carrying on multiple new war activities as well as the normal TVA program. Ordnance plants using TVA power were at work all over the Valley, and Lilienthal could say in an aside to TVA employees, as he conveyed the War Department's thanks, "Suppose the power situation had been handled as the rubber situation was handled. What in hell do you think we would be making airplanes out of today?"

War needs used, not power alone, but every one of TVA's multiple activities. River traffic was real and important, with barges carrying pig iron from Birmingham and grain from the Middle West, and shipbuilding started in the river ports. The TVA demountable houses that had been innovations at Hiwassee were being copied for defense housing over the country. The normal TVA farm program was expanded because of the need to help wartime production, with serious attention paid to the experiments with dehydrated foods that TVA had undertaken long before.

Under war pressure there was new collaboration with private industry, and in return for TVA operation of Alcoa dams on the Little Tennessee, which would function more economically as part of the TVA system, the Authority gained the Fontana dam site which had long been an important objective. Lilienthal called the unique agreement, between a privately owned system and a public agency, "one of the most important developments in relations between government and business in our time.'

People who dated world changes from the great industrial expansion of the United States during the first World War should note that, in the second, the power production of TVA was equal to half the production of the whole country in World War I. The TVA construction program was the largest single construction program ever undertaken in the country. Lilienthal remarked that it was "as if you were building eight Boulder dams at one time," or, in terms of men on the job, as if you were building three Grand Coulees.

With more people than most civilian agencies of the government, and with top war responsibilities—the Coast Guard set a watch on the dams—TVA did its expected wartime duty and volunteered for more. William Batt of WPB was to praise Lilienthal's "management perception" on the basis of war promises kept: "If they said that you could get so many thousand kilowatts of power at a given time from a given area, the chances were that you could depend on that promise, and they would deliver."

Before the war was over TVA was to get annual power production up to nearly 12 billion kilowatt-hours. Muscle Shoals would produce, besides elemental phosphorus, and ammonium nitrate for munitions and fertilizer, calcium carbide for synthetic rubber. TVA research projects, from food products to clays for spark plugs, took on new usefulness.

And in 1943, with TVA at the peak of wartime activity, David Lilienthal rolled up his sleeves and wrote a book.

He didn't take time off to do it; he got up at five in the mornings and wrote in shorthand, a short cut he learned, like Bernard Shaw, to save his time. And as he said in a speech to TVA dam builders, "Why in hell shouldn't we work hard? This is your country and mine that is fighting. We are not spectators in a war between other countries. It is our necks that are out." The book was part of Lilienthal's war effort; to others besides TVA employees, the TVA chairman had things to say.

He put in all the facts he had wanted in 1933, and had gathered for himself in ten years. But he didn't forget people. "TVA is people," said one of the sentences in the book, as easy to quote as "A river has no politics." *TVA · Democracy on the March* is so full of good quotations that ever since it appeared it has been hard for anybody to write about TVA without pilfering from it. It seems, too, that TVA has a peculiar literary influence. Everybody who writes about the Tennessee River, which rises where they still talk Elizabethan and runs through the Southern novel country, takes on a way of writing as recognizable as the house architecture named for the stylish Hudson. Lilienthal catches the rhythm of the river, but he says exactly what he wants to say, too; and of all the group of government men who were writing books, in the most literate administration since Jefferson's, Lilienthal's is most distinctly his own.

Certainly no other book about a government agency ever had the astonishing success this book has had. Translations, so far, number twenty—definitely including the Scandinavian, for Norway and Sweden have been greatly interested in TVA. High up on a shelf of Lilienthal's study are French, Spanish, Chinese, Italian, German translations, an English edition, and one published for Palestine; after that he lost count. He is proudest, and rightly, of the two-bit paper-bound edition you can buy in drugstores or on subway newsstands.

You could, of course, attribute the big sale of the book to the fact that the war made people see TVA as a necessity for the whole country, not just a help to the South. Slick-paper magazines published articles not attacking the Authority, as had been customary, but bragging on its war record. Conservative newspapers wrote approving editorials; Miss Dorothy Thompson, who had once written a whole row of columns stoutly opposing TVA, called it "the greatest constructive achievement of the New Deal." It looked as if most of the country agreed with Senator Norris when, on the Authority's tenth birthday, he sent a message saying that not only was there progress toward happiness and comfort and profit for the people of the South, as had been planned, but that here was "one of the most wonderful successes of all time."

Important evidence of that success, if you knew the Valley, were the "anniversary editions" of newspapers—not only in the cities but in the smaller towns—that carried congratulatory advertising from people who, in many cases, had once opposed the Authority as a menace to the taxpayers. Down in Huntsville, Alabama, only five years before, you could walk around the courthouse square with the white marble Confederate officer in the center, and if you asked in every store you wouldn't find one where they were willing to come out and say a good word for the new government agency. Over in the county agent's office they weren't showing any enthusiasm either. But in 1943 the Huntsville Chamber of Commerce paid for a full-page advertisement calling on all good citizens to protest against Senator McKellar's bill designed to hamstring TVA. "Farmers, this is your fight too!" said the big type.

Though he didn't mention these things in his book, Lilienthal couldn't help recording the triumphant accomplishments of TVA, and it turned out that his good news of people working together was what people everywhere wanted to read. He hadn't made a direct appeal to a world audience; he had only set out to answer, simply and directly, some of the questions that were coming in. These questions usually had to do with one special phase of TVA activity—power or reforestation or malaria control—and he wanted to show the over-all plan.

But publication of *TVA: Democracy on the March* didn't stop the inquiries that came in from all over the world; it added to them, and now they were addressed not to "TVA, Knoxville, U.S.A.," but to David Lilienthal himself. They were letters you had to answer because they showed people in desperate trouble thinking hopefully of a way that might mean salvation:

To the Chairman of the Tennessee Valley Authority

Dear Mr. Lilienthal:

We are writing to you from wartorn Greece. We are a group of young Greek engineers, architects, builders, teachers, and farmers. The last six years of our lives we have spent in war. We fought for liberty with zeal because we believed in the great democratic leaders, F. D. Roosevelt, W. Churchill, and the Atlantic charter.

Sixteen months have passed from the date of the liberation of our country. The huge work of reconstruction has not started yet. In the poor villages of Greece, thousands of farmers have lost what homes they had, they were burned by the Italians and the Germans, they have lost their implements and they are crowding into the cities looking for food, repeating the well-known battle cry of our fathers "Greece is a poor country."

Greece is not poorer than Tennessee ten years ago. That is our motto.

We have here the same valleys, rivers, hills, and mountains as any other country in the world. We have estimated that our rivers will yield a minimum of four billion kilowatt hours when harnessed. Prewar we were using six hundred million kilowatt hours, 95 per cent of which was thermally produced with fuel 100 per cent imported.

We have a population of approximately seven million people, 70 per cent of which are occupied in farming, with old methods. Most of our villages are up in the mountains, far from any road, and have never heard of electricity. We have very rich natural resources in minerals. Bauxite, iron ore, magnesium, and many other ores have always been exported from Greece and returned in the form of products at exorbitant prices. Malaria has always been the curse of our farmer population. Arid land, eroded land has reduced our small cultivable areas to a dangerous minimum.

But we are not discouraged yet. We believe that we can achieve a better tomorrow for Greece and thus, in our small part, for the world by applying scientific knowledge to develop our natural resources. We want to do it in your way: "Resource development to be governed by the unity of nature herself." And we want the people to participate actively in that development.

This is why we are writing to you.

This letter is signed by five Athens teachers with various interests—one electrical engineer, one agronomist, one architect; one has a string of American college degrees, and one is a woman.

From France comes another letter describing war damage and explaining French need in terms of two wars and their aftermath. A literal translation in the TVA files reads:

As chief engineer of the Society Omnium Lyonnais in Paris, I actively participate in the hydroelectric equipment of France. I am as convinced as you that we must work the natural hydraulic resources, not only in the narrow purpose of selling electric force, but for improving in the larger scale the conditions of the human life.

The present situation in France must seem to you as very open to criticism. As I have an opportunity I would like to tell you how we have come down to this bad condition. It is necessary to know exactly what things are, to be able to judge them.

The 1914-1918 war caused the death of 1,500,000 Frenchmen. An equal number died afterwards or were unable to work from the effects of the war. That makes a total of three million losses among the best. As you can see, that is a great number in proportion of forty million inhabitants.

During the period between the two wars, France laboriously recovered from their heavy losses and of the devastated regions which had to be rebuilt. During this time, Germany was increasing her industrial power with the help of the investments that your financiers lent to her and that were never given back. so that, in 1940, France was unable alone to stand the shock of the powerful German armies and she collapsed.

During the occupation, and chiefly during the liberation, the economical and industrial equipment was almost entirely destroyed. The destruction began with the Allied bombardment, was continued by the Germans when they left, and completed by the action of the French Resistance. And, once more, we have over one million dead.

It is with such distressful material that we have to rebuild our country. Besides, as it is after every war, and especially every occupation, the morality of the French people sank to a lower level. . . .

In such a crisis the application of such principles as those which gave rise to the TVA appears to me as the best way for the national straightening. . . .

It is interesting to see how many letter writers, particularly those who write to David Lilienthal the author, or those who have been to the Valley and seen TVA in action, emphasize not the huge achievements of the Authority but its way of working—what the French engineer called its principles. Another French engineer, who had talked to Lilienthal on his trip to Tennessee, wrote

Your point of view and the practices of TVA are so different from what we are accustomed to that I have given to them a very careful attention. I have written a small report on them.

In the past, I have had a tendency to favor and to emphasize co-ordination and centralization, but in the future, because of what you told me, I might very well steer away from this tendency.

The letters came from governments and from individuals. They came from China, India, Central and South America, Australia, Africa; from Sweden, Norway, Siam, Switzerland, Eire; from Iran, Yugoslavia, Mexico, Canada, Egypt. They came from both sides of the political fence. There are left-wingers and royal commissioners and numbers of businessmen anxious to find out how TVA stimulates the growth of industry. It is interesting to see how the inquiries, ranging over the fields covered by TVA's multipurpose activities, reflect the varying national needs. The Indians ask about refrigeration, malaria control, and co-operation with local or "village" authorities. The South Americans want to know how to harness rivers, the Dutch ask about land reclamation, the Chinese want erosion control and reforestation. A man in New South Wales asks about TVA library service. There is "tremendous interest" in Australia. Specific proposals are made for "our own TVA" in spots all over the world—in Kenya, in Scotland, on the Saskatchewan, on the Jordan. Exiled Spanish republicans write from Mexico and France to say what they plan to do on the Ebro, while a Franco man comes over to look around. A president of Colombia was elected on a "TVA for Colombia" platform, and President Alemán of Mexico is a TVA enthusiast.

Not all of these foreign fans read Lilienthal's widely translated book *TVA: Democracy on the March*. Some saw films or listened to OWI broadcasts or heard speeches by American ambassadors called on to explain what TVA meant. But when foreigners look across the world and write a letter to ask about TVA, they tend to address the chairman. As one letter puts it, "I think Mr. Lilienthal's name is known to people of Wales who could not say what the name of the British Prime Minister is." And from China: "We who study regional economics in China regard your name and TVA as the same thing because the one cannot be separated from the other."

A Congressman wrote to Lilienthal, forwarding an inquiry from Turkey: "Of all the things about which people in authority made inquiry during my sojourn in twenty-one countries, the most frequent was concerning the TVA. This was true in India, in Syria, in Lebanon, in Turkey, in Palestine, in Egypt, in Greece, and other spots." There are letters from people in Australia or China or some other far corner who write because they heard about TVA from Americans in the war, and they link TVA with winning the war. "It can safely be said," observes an Australian, "that without the enormous amounts of available electrical energy in Tennessee and other parts of U.S.A., the World War would not have been brought to a conclusion for several years, so that your work in TVA has had a beneficial effect on the whole world."

The principle of unity, stressed over and over in the book, was stretched to cover not the seven Valley states but all countries, as Indian visitors observed TVA's way with small rural co-operatives and applied it to the problems of Indian villages, or Chinese looked at the dams and moved them, in their imagination, to the rivers of their own country. As one wrote, "Most of Chinese are interested in TVA's yesterday, today, and tomorrow because China is now going to build our own TVA."

The fact is that TVA achievement was recognized abroad, as prophets and forward-looking movements often are recognized, before it was appreciated at home. Back in the days of the Wisconsin Power Commission, David Lilienthal made a speech in Lansing, Michigan, on the same program with a professor from the London School of Economics who was there to talk of the problems of English cities in the depression that followed the first World War. Not because of personal friendship so begun, but because of what happened in the Tennessee Valley in the next five years, the two men met again; in 1937 Doctor Herman Finer came back to this country with an assignment from the International Labor Office to write a book about TVA.

This was not the first foreign study or even the first foreign book to appear; in 1936 Odette Keun, the French woman journalist, had written a quick but penetrating little book, and there had been innumerable scientific or popular articles. Dr. Finer's book, however, was a thorough

[ 103 ]

job, representing several years of observation and considering TVA methods as they applied to countries all over the world. Dr. Finer wrote that

The world is full, as the Tennessee Valley was full, of as yet unexploited or not fully exploited industrial opportunities and the auxiliary transport and distributive facilities. There are mineral resources, agricultural possibilities, and underemployed labour power all over the world awaiting utilization. . . .

As with the TVA, the international problem is not merely one of the discovery and exploitation of resources, but of making them available. As the TVA has proved valuable, instead of harmful, to the whole of the United States of America, international development works may play the same part in the world economy at large.

Dr. Finer took particular note of the "multipurpose" program, although he observed that for certain places a single application of TVA technique, such as milk processing, might be enough; but he saw the importance of integrated services where the

direct object was not only the development of a river and the land, but also the development of men and women. . . . So, also the execution of development works in certain underdeveloped countries may be quite impossible without health provisions—housing, sanitary works, hospitals, doctors, nurses, inspectors, etc. Recent experience in Brazil, Ecuador, Bolivia and Haiti emphatically confirms this point. . .

The important lesson to be learned from the regional aspect of the TVA is that existing political divisions of the world and their frontiers, whether States or their subdivisions, are not self-sufficient economic units. For resource development the proper area may be less than a square mile (a mine), or it may embrace a whole continent (for transport or power).

This was the balanced academic view, and important. But it was Lilienthal's book that made the people in drugstores understand that TVA was a whooping world-wide wonder.

The TVA proof that power well managed could mean useful work, a beautiful food-growing countryside, and happy people was exactly what was needed to restore the hope of a devastated world. Even while the power of the dams was going into the war, processing more than half the aluminum used for planes, the idea of TVA was beginning to build for peace. Some TVA energy, a sort of token installment of it, began going into gadgets for peace-time reclamation outside the Valley. There is plenty of rainfall from the Smokies to the Shoals, but experimenters at the University of Tennessee began working on a mechanical "rainmaker" for lands in need of irrigation.

Even the speed of war did not wreck the TVA way of doing things thoroughly and well. At Douglas dam, built under tremendous pressure when the power shortage was worst, the heartbreaking handicaps included two river floods. "Construction men," said Lilienthal in his speech of congratulation afterward, "have told me that they have never seen a setup harder on the physical endurance and spirit of workers." Yet cofferdams held and records were broken once more. At Fontana, the tallest dam east of the

[ 105 ]

Rockies was going up with the usual TVA construction village complete with library, and housing good enough to be turned into a recreation center after the war. A newspaperman noticed with the customary surprise that six thousand people were working there with "no honky-tonks, no bagnios, none of the riffraff which so often attends a giant construction project. There are none of the social phenomena which made Fort Peck, Grand Coulee, and some other construction jobs a stench in the nostrils of decent people and which are making the Army construction jobs in the Tennessee Valley a moral scandal even now."

As the power went out into more and more war materials, with TVA skill at map making applied to plotting the invasion fronts for both Europe and Asia, people began to wonder what would happen to this tremendous concentration of power, come peace. Mr. R. L. Duffus of the New York *Times* asked David Lilienthal about that —wouldn't there, again, be too much power in the Valley? But as usual, Lilienthal wouldn't agree. "You can't get too much energy," he said. "Use it and you create a demand for more. Energy isn't a commodity. It's an ever recurring cycle. The power of the dams flows into men's lives. It flows out again in the form of creative work. There's no end to it that I can see."

To most people it looked as if the peacetime part of the cycle would come around as it had been before, with TVA furnishing more power to light homes and run industry, some of the war industries in the Valley converting to peace jobs, and rates going down as use went up in the regular way. You could figure that people who favored TVA would talk about how many millions in flood damage had been saved at Chattanooga, while Edison Electric Institute would tell the papers that TVA was operating at a loss. The fight to abolish the poll tax would resume, and industrial demands might even up the freight rate. More and more people would drive down through the Smokies and go fishing in the Norris lake or sailing at Guntersville, and gaze admiringly at Fontana, the blue-eyed glamour girl of all the TVA dams.

Much of this has now come to pass. Pick up a Southern paper and you see it in the headlines—Georgia teachers are striking for more pay, while Alabama schools are getting more revenue. Tennessee is hoping for a hundred-million-dollar industrial investment this year. They're going to make nylons at Chattanooga. They're flying air freight from the mills at Huntsville, Alabama. A Monroe County farmer, thanks to TVA phosphates, is making twenty-five dollars an acre on lespedeza. More tourists than ever are riding through the TVA estates to see the reconstructed South, wearing green velvet cover crops and her new reservoir sapphires, and looking like a lady again.

You could be sure, too, before the war ended, that David Lilienthal could go on being chairman of TVA the way Roosevelt went on being President. His handling of the biggest construction job of the war could have taken him in other directions; at about the time David Junior got old enough to join the Navy and head for Honolulu, there was a report from conquered Berlin that his father might

[ 107 ]

be called on to follow Eisenhower as head of the American military government in Germany. But Lilienthal always said TVA was his first love and he'd stick by her.

So forty days before he died, President Roosevelt wrote this letter to Representative Estes Kefauver of Tennessee:

THE WHITE HOUSE

Washington
March 2, 1945

Dear Estes:

It was good to have your letter about David Lilienthal. You may be sure that nothing in my administration has given me more satisfaction than the manner in which the TVA plan has been developed under his leadership in such a way as to create a pattern for the most productive relationship between people and their resources.

I have, of course, been gratified to watch the growth of enthusiasm in this country and abroad for TVA. You and I can remember when TVA was denounced as one of this administration's wild ideas. It does not seem wild now even to many of those who damned it most loudly at first. But it is, as it was, a great American idea. It is still disturbing, of course, to old advocates of the exploitation of resources without much concern for people beside them. It still disturbs, too, those who do not understand the meaning of TVA as an instrument by which big government need not be absentee government.

TVA, under David Lilienthal, has shown all of us that great national powers can be exercised as government at hand, at home, working with the people and their local governments where the people are. In the wider development of that understanding we shall continue to need such courage and vision as

David Lilienthal has shown in the Valley of the Tennessee to the nation and to the world.

Very sincerely yours,
Franklin D. Roosevelt

Honorable Estes Kefauver
House of Representatives
Washington, D. C.

With that recommendation it was clear that David Lilienthal could go on working for TVA even under a new President. But there were things going on in the Valley that would change the way of life in the whole world after the war.

It began when the government took over a big tract of land near Clinton, in the Smokies, and began moving people out. The Army Engineers weren't as gentle about that as the TVA relocation men had been, and surprised farmers appealed to TVA for help in finding new places to live. Then the government asked TVA about housing for large numbers of industrial workers coming in, and for power—immense amounts of power, to be provided by the new Fontana dam. Nobody knew what they were making at Clinton. Some politically minded humorists said Roosevelt buttons for the next campaign. Others, mindful of old legends lingering in the mist-ridden hills, said silver bullets that would end the war. It was true that the Government loaned itself millions in mint silver to use instead of the scarcer copper in one of the new plants.

Whatever they were doing, they were using power. Years later, Jennings Perry quoted TVA's fish expert on one of the little ways in which it showed: "We had the devil of a time," Dr. Eschmeyer said at Norris, "keeping the atom secret here. All the fishermen would keep asking why we were pulling down the level of the lake out of season. It was to furnish big blocks of power to Oak Ridge, of course. But I'd have to make up something else to tell them."

David Lilienthal has said that he knew no more than anybody else about what complicated scientific work was going on, although he could no longer claim that he lacked a doctor's degree—DePauw, in the spring of 1945, gave him one. But that year's more important commencement was at Radcliffe, where his daughter Nancy, who had worked at Oak Ridge during the summer of 1944, was getting an A.B. *cum laude* in economics. Her father said in the commencement address:

The great issue of our time, with which you and your generation will be at grips day in and day out for the rest of your lives, is simply this: Are machines to control men, or are men to control machines and direct them for the glory of God and the flowering of the human spirit?

He went on to contrast the view of the people who hate gadgets—"they are homesick for a simpler life"—with that of the worshipers of the machines that "produce more and more things," that "provide new sensations, sensations of speed and motion and power, the excitement of new buttons to press." Neither, he warned the New England girl graduates, was right:

The machine is neither good nor evil in itself. It is good only when man uses it for good. It is evil only if he puts it to evil purposes.

The machine can, of course, be used to degrade or enslave man. It can destroy the countryside.

But that would happen, the speaker said, only if men themselves chose to have it so. He went on to cite the warning of the Czech play, *R.U.R.*:

But we are not robots. Science and the skills of management, the constantly wider understanding of *how* to get things done —these add up to the conclusion that we can deliberately and consciously direct and shape the course of events.

This speech of course applied to the things TVA was known to be doing to finish up the war, but it meant even more than the Radcliffe girls or even Nancy Lilienthal's father could have known. In two months more, the bomb was dropped on Hiroshima and the little Oak Ridge paper came out with what they were doing at Clinton: "Oak Ridge Attacks Japanese."

There it was at last, the worst that TVA power could do—or the best, if you looked at it in terms of bringing the war to a speedy end. But here, sure enough, was energy for David Lilienthal to think about using. Here, where the world was looking for a blueprint for peace, TVA had powered the biggest threat to the future ever seen. It looked almost as if the war wasn't over after all, or as if there might be a long struggle to make the power that worked for war work for peace without destruction. There was a peace that you couldn't call a peace, and no discharge in that war.

In the war years Bernard Shaw had paid the Authority a great compliment: he said war was required to make some people work fast, but TVA had the secret of work in peacetime. Now that secret would be the world's big need, to offset what people were calling the secret of atomic energy.

# VII

*"The appointment of Mr. Lilienthal to the Atomic Energy Commission is something that only God himself can explain."*

Representative EUGENE COX of Georgia,
in House of Representatives, April, 1947.

TEN YEARS AGO two counties northeast of Knoxville were the problem children, and the pride, of TVA. Roane and Anderson counties had poor land but good people. The land was so tired out it took fertilizer even to grow a cover crop. There were gullies everywhere and there was no money to stop them. But the people were better educated than some, and willing to do what they could. So TVA made surveys and went to work, and soon there were demonstration farms all over the area, with the farmers taking advice about terracing and crop rotation, and using TVA phosphates. The little town of Wheat turned itself into a willing guinea pig to show what a farm community co-operating with the TVA program could do.

By the war years, Wheat community and the surrounding farmland had come a long way. The people were proud and TVA was proud. They weren't exactly prepared for what happened to them when the Army moved into Roane and Anderson counties to set up the Clinton Engineering

[ 113 ]

District, turning out the farmers and ploughing up the fields to found the town of Oak Ridge. You could see why the Army engineers chose that place; on three sides of the district a horseshoe bend of the Clinch River makes a natural moat. On the fourth side, Black Oak Ridge gave the new war boom town its name.

Now, where the demonstration farms used to be, visitors can buy little two-bit pennants lettered "Oak Ridge—Home of the Atomic Bomb." Long after the war's end, visitors to Oak Ridge also discovered that the Army was still in control.

The end of the war boom reduced the Oak Ridge population by half, but with only forty thousand people left the guess was that because of processing improvements, fissionable material was being made at an increasing, not declining, rate. In 1946, in spite of the housing—prefabs, trailers, and dormitories—there were signs of permanence. Duckboards were being replaced by sidewalks and concrete gutters were going into place along the red-clay gullies. Buildings and barracks that had been khaki colored were freshly painted white or yellow, and the dust-brown area buses turned red and white. Pioneers liked to recall the bulldozer and hip boots period, only three years before, but civic boosters had a Lions Club which advertised a "Turtle Derby"—favorite sport of Southern cities—on the high-school football field.

Like the rest of the country, Oak Ridge was wondering about its job, come peace. It wasn't too well rooted in Tennessee; near-by Knoxville had got resigned to TVA, but another invasion in ten years, with a war boom too, was too much.

As Yankees would, they had called the atom-smashing enterprise the Manhattan Project. Laying out the Oak Ridge streets, they marked a Broadway running catty-cornered through the town. There was a Pennsylvania Avenue, a California Avenue, a Vermont Avenue; and branching off Vermont, a Vienna Road.

As far as planning went they did well, learning from the TVA construction. For reasons of safety they hid the factories, so you could live for days in Oak Ridge and not see one. They built a convenient community center, with a town library and a bookmobile, TVA style, and three churches to rotate denominational services as in the early days at Norris. They built good schools and playgrounds and a million-dollar hospital. The Army kept the streets clean and the health record good.

They even did their best not to show Army control. The Roane-Anderson Company, a subsidiary of a New York construction company, was formed for the sole purpose of administering Oak Ridge. The Roane-Anderson Company then set up its own subsidiaries to handle housing, and granted concessions for transportation, shops, and so forth. In practice the Oak Ridgers dealt with the Galbraith-Moore Company or the Ridenour Company (handling Negro housing) when they paid their rent, the A & P when they bought groceries, and so on.

Nevertheless the town was under military control, or industrial control with the Army sitting on top. Suppose there was a shortage of housing: who would decide what sort of house a worker was entitled to rent? For Army officers the question was settled by rank, and similarly the top-ranking men in industry had to be taken care of—you couldn't ask a man to come to Oak Ridge unless you gave him a decent roof over his head. On lower levels the authorities did consider the number of children in a family, as in veterans' housing, and perhaps for this reason the Oak Ridge birth rate was high. But if you lost or quit your job, of course you lost your house.

This was like any company town, except that the Army was over the industrial plants. If the companies had been just one big company, the Oak Ridge resident would have been living in a corporate state. And although employing companies were three, Tennessee Eastman, Carbide and Carbon, and Monsanto Chemical, for the farmer turned factory hand the choice was between the first two, since Monsanto ran a research laboratory employing scientists.

So the war set up in three years, in the fields where they had learned to grow lespedeza, a town that was socially planned but military in administration. The Army, under the red flag of the engineers, did a good job in its way. Of all people employed at Oak Ridge the Army appeared happiest in professional acceptance of Oak Ridge destiny. "Praise the Lord and pass the ammunition," sang the 'teen-age MP at the Edgemoor gate, inspecting passes. The sergeant driver of a press car was grieved to hear anyone question the wisdom of using the bomb over Japan. He felt it to be the perfect and necessary answer to Pearl Harbor. More on his mind was the fact that the Army at Oak Ridge was in the curious position of using TVA power—

after a long feud with TVA over who should build the dams—to make atom bombs employed, at the moment, to further the shipbuilding plans of the Navy.

But to Americans, Army administration of a big civilian town doesn't seem natural or right. Individual liberty in Oak Ridge seemed to narrow down to a choice between film and radio programs, planting zinnias or marigolds by the trailer steps, or taking turnip greens instead of hominy at the cafeteria. The more stubborn individualists could still argue for personal responsibility and say, of the difference between zinnias and no zinnias, "It's the folks. Some plant things if they know they're gonna leave; others won't even if they're stayin'." But to most people, especially those going in and out of town, to the hills or to Knoxville, it seemed wrong to have to show a military pass on every road, wrong to be working in peacetime for even a good-natured Army.

Going deeper than such surface annoyances, or even the uncertainty about jobs that was felt all over the country, was the Oak Ridge sense of doubt about the work in hand. There the difference between Oak Ridge and a TVA construction town was plainest. The TVA towns were engaged in helpful, constructive work, and everyone from driller to chief engineer could look at a growing dam and smile with pride. Oak Ridge, like all America, was both proud and ashamed of the bomb; people supposed that, to win the war, it was necessary. But it was hard to feel pride over a growing stockpile of material for more bombs.

When the great news broke back in the summer of '45, a worker in the Carbide plant was quoted as saying, "Looks

[ 117 ]

like we got to find a way to stop the next war, sure." That was in the first flush of power when anything seemed possible. Later, in the fear of layoffs, some plant workers stopped worrying over the possibility of another war; one AFL organizer said, "I don't want to talk about it—I've got a son old enough to be in it, next time. But *we* can't do nothin' about it—*they're* gonna decide, the people that run things." Waiting for a bus, an ex-GI said, "I'd just as soon we hadena busted that atom—now it looks like we got a tiger by the tail."

Oak Ridge was different from TVA towns in another way: it could boast not only good working people and top-flight engineers but a big middle class made up of minor scientists who were well-educated white-collar workers. These young scientists and their wives were self-conscious and restless. They amused themselves with "Summer Pops," concerts of recorded music, and organized their own orchestra. They started a little theater and persuaded the famous Barter Theatre to come over from Virginia, to play *Blithe Spirit, State of the Union* and *Wings over Europe.* Wives organized a League of Women Voters that started trying to make the town think about a town council, which would be useful if and when the Army went.

The young scientists also liked to talk among themselves, mainly about international affairs. In these discussions their religious and educational backgrounds played a part; some were naturally anti-Russian, others thought that scientists should set up a priesthood keeping itself above political thought, others still were plain worried about where a growing accumulation of fissionable material would lead the world. Yet above all questions of politics and of conscience they had an intense practical interest in their jobs, and would argue at the drop of a hat about processes and whether or not Y-25 was already obsolete.

Even with this white-collar group to talk and the workers themselves worried, there wasn't anything like a general case of jitters. With the rest of the country Oak Ridge went home from work to compete for scarce consumer goods, do a little bowling or root for the home team, and take turns baby sitting so the missus could go to the movies. About the time of the first Bikini test, a large sign appeared on Jackson Square which read "The Mind Is Destroyed in SHOCK." It referred to a film thriller at the Center Theater. If this seems like playing with pinwheels on top of a volcano, it may be mentioned that although private ownership of firecrackers is against the law, they did have a community fireworks display in Oak Ridge on July 4.

What Oak Ridge folks still like best of all is to go fishing. They fish on Sundays, going off with bamboo poles and buying live bait on sale at the edge of the town, and coming back proudly with strings of fish from as far away as the Norris reservoir. Besides supplying the power for a lethal industry the Clinch River is posted as a "Fishing Area—no small boats or fires allowed."

If they stayed home and read the papers they might be no better off. Under the Army, the little Oak Ridge *Journal* confined itself carefully to local items: "We print personal stories about people right here," the woman editor explained. "If they want outside news they can get it from the city papers." But the city paper most frequently seen, brought in from Knoxville, carried Pegler as its top feature. In line with its sensationalism a few Oak Ridgers said darkly, of the local output, "Looks like we might have to use 'em again."

In the drugstore a radio loud-speaker drew elderly listeners who would once have argued round a stove, and one shook his head angrily when the commentator said Henry Wallace wanted to give away the "bomb secret." Nevertheless, in a poll on world government taken in Oak Ridge in the spring of '45, sampling twelve hundred persons, it was found that three-fourths of them wanted a world government, a world bill of rights, atom control, and a world police force. Maybe David Lilienthal had this in mind when he said that he wasn't worried about Oak Ridge, he only hoped the rest of the South and of the country would do as well.

Or maybe he had in mind what the young people were doing in the Oak Ridge high school. Because Uncle Sam's money paid for them, the Oak Ridge schools started well above the average not only for Tennessee but for the country. Teachers gathered from all parts of the country worked to make sure that, despite the difficulty of free local action, youngsters growing up in Oak Ridge should know how democracy worked. They were given more than the usual opportunity to think for themselves in school, and the schools were from the start important to the town. During the boom period the junior high school had the second biggest enrollment in the country. The senior high school became famous for its Youth Council on the Atomic Crisis.

At Christmas, 1945, that young organization issued an appeal to students everywhere, to citizens, and to the government, to do something about the atom bomb. An editorial in the *Oak Leaf,* the school paper, was quoted in newspapers and on the air; it said:

"We wish that you could know Oak Ridge—know what it is to grow up almost in the shadow of these massive factories which can bring glory to the world or utter destruction. You would listen then when our scientists speak.

"To stop a war and save the lives of  millions, our fathers and our brothers made this bomb. It served its purpose well. Before Oak Ridge was, some of them labored long and hard to split the atom. In finding out its secrets, they learned full well its power for good and ill. While it remains unbridled, they fear this power. We share their fear.

"We have listened to those of them who are our scientists. We believe them. This is what they say: 'As scientists, we know the thing we've made. Here is titanic power to bring blessing undreamed of to our world—or to wreck it altogether. As scientists, we consider it probable that one person out of every three of you will one day die because of it.' Fathers would not say this to their children to deceive them.

"We do not want to die a needless death. . . . We want to realize the promise of atomic power. To do this freely, we must end its threat. . . .

"We wish to join our elders in a mandate to the govern-

[ 121 ]

ment of the United States so to govern us that atomic energy will henceforth be used only for peaceful, constructive purposes."

When they said "our fathers and our brothers made this bomb" the Oak Ridge students were not talking idly; during the war, only their first names could be mentioned in the school paper because their last names, some of them famous in science or on Army rolls, were military secrets. So their plea won attention; other schools wrote to ask about establishing their own councils, and student speakers from Oak Ridge went as far as Philadelphia and New York. At Philadelphia they held school forums, with questions and answers that the whole country needed to overhear:

Q.: Is the atom bomb more important than gunpowder in its day?

A.: Certainly. Atomic energy is useful not only for bombs but for industry and medicine.

Q.: Shouldn't the United States keep control of atomic energy?

A.: No, other countries are interested in helping their people. Some of us seem to think the earth is flat and ours is the only side of it. If we keep control too long, it will be disastrous to us. Other nations will discover it anyway.

Q.: How much do they know now?

A.: We asked scientists at Oak Ridge about that and they said it was like asking a boy if he could bake a cake. The boy may not know how to bake a cake but if he has the ingredients he can get hold of a cookbook and learn.

Q.: Must we give up our national sovereignty?

A.: Would we be giving up anything? Sovereignty is simply a

matter of who does the deciding. In the matter of war, as things stand now, we don't make the decisions anyway. *We* didn't decide to go to war in 1941. Adolf Hitler and Hirohito decided for us. Under a world government, the people would decide whether there would be war or peace. We would not be losing sovereignty but gaining it.

Q.: What about Russia?

A.: Russia doesn't think we're playing marbles with atom bombs.

Q.: Has Russia given us any reason to trust her? Can our scientists tour Russia?

A.: At Oak Ridge we didn't tell them to come in and look, either.

Q.: Do you look for social changes such as the industrial revolution which followed the use of steam?

A.: Atomic energy will revolutionize certain industries. We are living in a new age now—the year 1 A.B.

The first appeal to Lilienthal to consider the atomic energy problem had come some time before, when the Oak Ridge scientists, taking what was for scientific men an epochal step toward participation in world affairs, organized their own association and—as public and private organizations had often done—asked the TVA chairman for advice on administration. This was before atomic scientists of Chicago and Los Alamos joined with those of Oak Ridge to form the Federation of American Scientists, organized "to meet the increasingly apparent responsibility of scientists in promoting the welfare of mankind and the achievement of a permanent peace." It was also before

Lilienthal was made chairman of the committee of consultants on the State Department report.

In New York, the young president of YCAC, Joe Glasgow, made a speech at the *Herald Tribune* Forum on the same program with David Lilienthal. Joe was just about the age of the junior David, then in the Navy, and his father had been a relocation man for TVA. The two speeches, made together, brought TVA and Oak Ridge together before the public as they had been together all along. Lilienthal, speaking first, started by scaring the audience a little as it seems you have to, to make them think about atomic bombs. "You live in one of the world's most densely populated and closely built areas. You surely are aware of the utter havoc a few such bombs would bring to this wonderful city and its environs and to the ten million people who live in this immediate region."

The forum was called to talk about "The World We Want"; Lilienthal said plainly that a world that anyone would want would be impossible, with atomic warfare. "The two are contradictory. They can't exist together. And since from now on it seems inevitable that any major war will employ atomic weapons, this simply means we cannot have another war—not if we are to have the world we want."

The collective invention of the bomb, he suggested, called for a new social invention to match it. The United Nations was a social invention, the idea of police power—arming a few men so the rest could go unarmed—was another invention. Such social inventions called for general public understanding and application. "Physical discover-

[ 124 ]

ies can be made by a few men, or even one man—penicillin, let us say—and therefore their acceptance and use can come overnight. But social inventions—new ways of getting along together—if they are to be effective, must be understood by people generally and be acceptable to them."

Lilienthal mentioned briefly the plan for atomic energy control on which his own committee had been at work for the State Department—"you might call the report and the plan an anti-suicide pact." Then he compared the prospects for successful atomic control with the successful application of technical knowledge that, through twenty-six TVA dams, "controls floods that in time past have caused great human suffering. Turbines and generators now produce electricity out of waters that once drowned men and destroyed their homes." This enabled him to end on a note of hope for the audience of students:

True, that electricity which like atomic energy can be either a constructive or a destructive force, travels over transmission lines to the huge plant at Oak Ridge, where it helps to make the material of atomic bombs. But electricity from the very same dam also goes down country roads to pump the water, saw the wood and do much of the drudgery on many farms. What I am saying by this illustration from our Valley is this: whether science and technology work for man's good or his destruction is up to us. Your generation will have no more difficult and at the same time no more fruitful issue with which to deal.

Young Richard Joseph Glasgow of Oak Ridge, following, insisted on bringing the Manhattan Project home to

[ 125 ]

Manhattan. "We are Americans from all over the United States, living in an American town. You may think we are different because we live with the mighty question that has made our town a symbol of terror and of hope. There is no cause for difference, the question is just as close to you."

Nobody realized, at that time, what the Lilienthal Committee report dated March 16, 1946, was to mean; but people were concerned about the fight in Congress over civilian versus military control of atomic energy. Congressman May of Kentucky, still head of the House Committee on Military Affairs, was for military control. Senator McMahon of Connecticut was for civilian control, and he had the backing of scientists in Los Alamos and Chicago—Oppenheimer, Urey, Szilard, Fermi—and also, of course, the Oak Ridge scientists. He even had the enthusiastic support of high-school students in Oak Ridge.

In Congress familiar arguments were advanced. For the Committee on Un-American Activities, Representative J. Parnell Thomas of New Jersey read a report of an investigator at Oak Ridge who regarded as subversive the fact that members of scientific societies there were "very active in support of international civilian control" of atomic materials, and "devoted to the creation of some form of world government," also that they were willing to "admit communication with persons outside the United States." Representative Rankin of Mississippi followed with a charge that Communists were "packed into every department of this government" including the War Department, and that "the first thing you know our people will be blown to pieces by this atomic bomb."

Despite these considerations and the active legislative opposition of Mr. May, the McMahon bill was passed and Oak Ridge heaved a sigh of relief. There was more tension, though, as weeks and months passed without appointment of the civilian commission provided for in the bill. In Washington, the Lilienthal committee was praised for the report which had furnished a basis for the Baruch report to the United Nations; but in Oak Ridge the first anniversary of Hiroshima passed without determination of the question in everybody's mind.

When school started the YCAC met and, at a discussion in the neon-lit school library, students swapped questions with parents, teachers, and scientists:

"Is the United States becoming a militaristic nation?" "If we were to fight Russia right now, could we win?" "Would it be Christian to attack Russia?" "Are we a Christian nation anyhow?" "Considering the representatives from this state, can anything be done with Congress?" And the question that hurt most: "Why, with no plans for international inspection, do we keep on stockpiling materials here in Oak Ridge?"

The town couldn't be happy because, even with the McMahon bill passed and the Army slated to go, so much would depend on the sort of administration that would follow. There could be a civilian administration, so called, that would do away with certain Army efficiencies and provide nothing better. In that case you could be sure that in five years Oak Ridge would be just a Southern mill town. Housing and public services would deteriorate until you had something like another Kingsport, Tennessee, or

Bethlehem, Pennsylvania. With the state of Tennessee unable to pay the salaries of a Columbia-trained school superintendent and his staff, an early casualty would be the school system.

And of course there would be no losing the Army as chief customer of the industrial plants. With a weak civilian administration this would mean remote control, but plants working on Army orders would have an excuse to put no-strike clauses into union contracts.

Not that Oak Ridge did much direct worrying about strikes or unions. Maybe the workers should have been more excited about the organizing drive of the two unions, the Atom Workers' Organizing Committee, CIO, and the Atomic Workers' Council, AFL. But even before the election it was safely predicted that majority sentiment was for no union; a poll had already shown an overwhelming percentage in favor of a no-strike vote in A-bomb factories.

Union campaigns followed characteristic patterns. CIO rented nice clean offices in Galesburg Hall, the converted dormitory that is Oak Ridge's best business block. It had as organizer a former TVA man, and its office bookshelf boasted probably the only copy of Odum's *The Southern Regions* to be found outside the school and the town library. It published its own paper during the campaign.

AFL headquarters in the Gamble Valley trailer camp seemed more like a Tammany hangout. Knoxville-printed literature obtainable there stressed the personal-vituperation note still popular with Southern reaction. The most effective AFL argument was against CIO as a "foreign" organization, with organizers "named by some damn Yankee up North."

Chief embarrassment to both unions was the fact that Oak Ridge workers were well paid—neither union dared raise the wage issue—and much more concerned with keeping their jobs than with wages or grievances. The CIO paper attacked AFL on the ground that an AFL strike had been called in a Monsanto plant in Illinois, thus appealing for support on an implied no-strike pledge. The CIO also maintained friendly relations with the Army engineers. AFL thundered against the "determined, dictatorial, undemocratic and un-American policy of the Army's higher authorities to deny the right of organizations to labor at Oak Ridge." It even hinted darkly at "underhanded and undercover arrangements . . . between the Army and the CIO." But these arguments failed to convince, and the Carbide and Carbon plant went CIO by 25 votes, 1918 to 1893.

But the biggest plant, Tennessee Eastman, went "No Union" and at any time you could raise more argument in Oak Ridge about religion than you could about the unions. At the white-painted Chapel on the Hill, they were reading, any Sunday, words at least as applicable to what was on the Oak Ridge mind as anything in the union literature:

"Thou turnest man to destruction. . . .

"And establish thou the work of our hands upon us; yea, the work of our hands establish thou it."

Underneath the worry about postwar jobs and food

prices and Congress was another worry, which in some degree affected the whole country but was centered at Oak Ridge. With its factories and its white-collar workers, its students and its scientists Oak Ridge was the whole country in miniature, with this exception: that the wartime changes had come fast, in sight, and been so sweeping that you couldn't forget them. A man who once had a peach orchard where the big Carbide and Carbon plant stood could look at it and wonder—as he did, a little bothered yet not in complete despair—whether what that plant was making would ever be as good as the fruit his peach trees bore.

Then the Valley papers printed something that was good news to everybody who knew anything about TVA, and that of course included Oak Ridge. They said that David Lilienthal would probably be named to head the civilian Atomic Energy Commission.

People in Oak Ridge knew what that could mean. It was true that some newcomers, such as a new CIO organizer, might ask what Mr. Lilienthal's attitude would be; but the scientists didn't have to ask, or the farmers who had left their work with TVA phosphates to help make fissionable material. The man who had owned the peach orchard knew and was glad. The people who were working to make Oak Ridge a town like any American town saw they'd have a chance.

So at Christmas, 1946, the YCAC editorial in the *Oak Leaf* was less despairing. It still faced the danger of atomic war, said:

Such war is unthinkable. Yet we must think of it. . . .

In such a war, thickly populated cities will be devastated in a manner that the most vivid imagination has difficulty to conceive. Industrial might and wealth will vanish, as rocket-propelled craft, carrying atomic warheads, plummet down far faster than sound can travel. Bombs, planted during the so-called peace preceding the sudden attack, will detonate, devastating great areas, which will be rendered poisonously radioactive, therefore uninhabitable. Those who, escaping the first attacks, take refuge from the atomic fire can still be reached by the equally scientific, equally frightful means of man-made pestilence. Famine, more extensive than any that Europe or Asia has ever known, will surely follow any large-scale use of the atomic bomb. But, if man wishes to use famine as a separate weapon, he can release crop destroying agencies to produce it. These are not nightmarish fancies. They are facts. This is what we mean now when we talk of the next war. It must not happen. Our faith is that it will not.

But the Oak Ridge young people spoke, too, with fervor and hope for modern man:

He whom Almighty God has given the power to know what is right and what is wrong surely . . . will see that all the different peoples of the world, before we, the younger ones, have seen many additional new years, must come together and live as one people, as citizens of the world; not as races, parties, or clashing nationalities.

And they asked for positive practical results:

Is a war-free world of united peoples an idealistic vision? Perhaps it is. But it is also a practical necessity, which can be

[ 131 ]

accomplished by practical means. We are a practical people who are accustomed to doing the hitherto impossible when we work together toward a common goal. What greater goal could a people have than this? When we can give each year to useful ends the effect that is represented by the billions of dollars that we are spending now for war, and when people everywhere can do the same, what need we lack? We can restore our wasted lands and make them yield plenty for us all. What we need we can have: food, clothing, shelter, medical care, education, leisure, travel, and universal friendship free of fear.

This is the promise of the atomic age. This man can have. Why need he be afraid? Here is good work for him to do. Let him now resolve to do it.

It was true that summer had passed and the harvest was ended and the country was not saved. Few people read the Lilienthal report, while many people knew of the fight against the Lilienthal appointment which Senator McKellar, according to his promise, was making. But lest Oak Ridge people grow too worried, David Lilienthal made a speech there in April, 1947. He talked in the high-school auditorium, and knowing that it would not hold the people who wanted to hear him, the electrical engineers who are plentiful in Oak Ridge rigged up a loud-speaker system that took in the big dining hall and just about the whole town.

He said what people knew he would say—talked about how Oak Ridge had a safety record, and how he hoped that meant something not only for the town but for world. He showed that he knew something of the local concern about housing and schools; he said:

To make atomic energy requires human energy of a very high order. For this is a new, challenging, pioneering effort. There is nothing old or routine about it. Human energies cannot reach a high point of effectiveness—particularly in the building of a new field of knowledge and a wholly new industry—unless the surroundings and conditions under which these human energies are developed are favorable for the best efforts of men and women.

People who listened carefully saw that what he said meant more than care for housing; it meant care to make Oak Ridge a city where you could live and lift up your head and be proud of your work, not just a place where you worked for a big company, doing something you couldn't understand or believe in, but that seemed like peacetime preparation for a war you hoped would never come.

Oak Ridge workers knew they would have to go on working at things they didn't understand, and trust to Congress who, Mr. Lilienthal reminded them, was boss. But they could feel confidence in the intentions of a man who said, "Only through long searching, study and common sense can the goal of all just men be reached—peace on earth." Because, besides common sense, he did mention a goal.

Some of the people who had been moved out of Wheat community came down from the mountains and got passes into Oak Ridge to hear that speech. They weren't Oak Ridge workers, but Oak Ridge was on what had been their land. So they felt they had a right to be there, and they said they were glad that they had come; they felt better about what was going on.

# VIII

*The atom bomb is here to stay,*
*Most scientists agree.*
*Oh yes, the bomb is here to stay,*
*The question is, Are We?*

English Digest

SHORTLY after the Oak Ridge students asked that something be done, the State Department appointed a committee, headed by Dean Acheson and including Dr. Bush and Dr. Conant as well as General Groves, to report on the atomic energy problem. The Acheson committee in turn named a group of consultants which had David Lilienthal as chairman, Dr. J. R. Oppenheimer, Dr. Charles A. Thomas of Monsanto, Harry A. Winne of General Electric, and Chester I. Barnard of the New Jersey Bell Telephone Company as members. The report of the Lilienthal committee, made for the Acheson committee and in turn transmitted to the State Department, became well known but not sufficiently known as the Acheson-Lilienthal report.

It was the Lilienthal committee which got on trains and planes and went from Oak Ridge to Los Alamos looking over the mystery plants, with a short lecture course by Dr. Oppenheimer on what it was all about. To begin with, the committee consisted of five men of widely differing backgrounds—a research scientist, two industrial engineers, and one executive officer from big corporations, and one man who had made his career in public service. That they should have come to unanimous agreement on a program, or even continued on good speaking terms while they were, as Mr. Barnard described it, "in constant contact," and "working daily, many nights a week, traveling on junkets by plane and train to various parts of the project," might have seemed too much to expect. When they did agree on a report, and one that offered a positive, apparently practical plan, the possible explanations were: that they were united in mutual awe of the atom, that they were browbeaten or hypnotized into agreement by the committee chairman, or that they were able to develop a plan so good as to deserve unanimous endorsement.

There is no doubt that they took the atom seriously. Dr. Oppenheimer told them what the students at Oak Ridge knew, and a little more. This information in its general aspects is summarized in the committee report, which therefore deserves study by legislators and voters the world over. In substance the conclusions are those which the student forums emphasized: "There is no secret. There is no defense. There must be international organization." If these conclusions seem clear and easy to remember, speeches in Congress, editorials in newspapers, and public opinions polls were to disclose that the very first of them was slow to penetrate the public mind.

To say "There is no secret" contradicts the simple American assumption that this is our bomb, we made it ourselves, and we can lock it up in the cupboard if we want to. The assumption, of course, overlooks the contributions made by other countries to research and the fact that leading American workers in atomic energy came to this country from abroad or went abroad for study. As the report put it,

... It is recognized that the basic science on which the release of atomic energy rests is essentially a world-wide science, and that in fact the principal findings required for the success of this project are well known to competent scientists throughout the world. It is recognized that the industry required and the technology developed for the realization of atomic weapons are the same industry and the same technology which play so essential a part in man's almost universal striving to improve his standard of living and his control of nature. It is further recognized that atomic energy plays so vital a part in contributing to the military power, to the possible economic welfare, and no doubt to the security of a nation, that the incentive to other nations to press their own developments is overwhelming.

Agreed, then, that the world must know or try to know, and so soon learn, the report went on to suggest using world interest for positive advantage:

... in the solution of this relatively concrete and most urgent problem of protecting mankind from the evils of atomic warfare, there has been created an opportunity for a collaborative approach to a problem which could not otherwise be solved, and the successful international solution of which would contribute immeasurably to the prevention of war and to the strengthening of the United Nations Organization. . . . There was hope and some reason to believe that in attempting to solve it, new patterns of cooperative effort could be established which would be capable of extension to other fields, and which might make a contribution toward the gradual achievement of a greater degree of community among the peoples of the world.

The alternate to this possible world co-operation, which assumed that nations might conceivably look at the situation and agree as the committee was agreeing, was the simple notion of "outlawing" atomic energy in warfare. Attractive as this was to American and to Russian isolationists, the report disposed of it briefly by pointing out that you cannot have unlimited use of atomic energy for peaceful industrial purposes without developing a war potential. Here the report does give a special credit to the United States: the "historically established reluctance of the United States to take the initiative in aggressive warfare" puts this country at a peculiar disadvantage in the case of surprise attack.

That inspection alone could prevent conversion of atomic energy development to war use was the next popular fallacy to be demolished. Here the report took a common-sense view of an old personnel problem: who will inspect the inspectors? Or, in the more polite language of the committee, where will you find for work which is "largely policing and auditing" the "very large and very highly qualified organization of experts and administrators needed"? You'd draw instead, the report said right out, "the kind of man who was attracted to prohibition squads."

[ 137 ]

Further, the report remarked, the very presence of a large number of "foreigners" empowered to snoop into industrial operations would in itself cause friction. A neat understatement suggested that this inspection of processes, places, and even of student scientists "would probably be as obnoxious to Americans as to any others." There would be unpleasant incidents, not only if inspectors were bribed or threatened, but if any nation could be accused of bribery or threats; and "such incidents could not be avoided." In other words, although a sensible approach to the problem of atomic energy control might conceivably unite national governments in a common cause, the effort to set up an international spy system would unquestionably cause trouble.

This section of the report concluded with a significant warning: "The raw materials of atomic energy, potentially valuable for new peacetime purposes and of critical importance for war, are already a matter of extreme competition between nations. The forces growing out of this situation and making for acute rivalry between nations seem to us far more powerful than those which cause the present rivalries with respect to such resources as oil."

A workable plan, said the committee, must first of all provide danger signals that would "flash early enough" to give time for actions against a nation making war. It must provide for the United States "a relatively secure position" should the plan fail. The plan must be flexible, to "cope with new dangers that must appear," and it must, while requiring international action, manage to minimize national rivalries. But the most important provision, in view of what was to follow, was that the plan must be one "that is not wholly negative, suppressive, and policelike." For,

We are not dealing simply with a military or scientific problem but with a problem in statecraft and the ways of the human spirit. Therefore the plan must be one that will tend to develop the beneficial possibilities of atomic energy and encourage the growth of fundamental knowledge, stirring the constructive and imaginative impulses of men rather than merely concentrating on the defensive and negative. It should, in short, be a plan that looks to the promise of man's future well-being as well as to his security.

Having outlined what looked like an impossible assignment, the committee began looking on the bright side. In the first place you could be thankful that the dreams of alchemy had not quite been achieved: you couldn't set up atomic-energy laboratories in the woodshed, with a few old bottles, and start turning clay or iron into fissionable material. Two materials, uranium and thorium, were the only ones so far useful in chain reactions, and thorium could be used only with uranium. More, "a vast scientific and industrial effort is necessary in order to produce atomic bombs." You could, therefore, for the present at least, concentrate on uranium supplies and look out for large industrial efforts.

But we weren't—remember—just going to police these danger spots, or dig a hole and "bury the whole idea . . . bury it deep . . . forget it." The obvious course would be to look hard at the possible uses, other than military, for the materials and the plants; and here the Lilienthal committee quoted another committee, one of scientists including A. H. Compton and Fermi in consultation with Rabi and Urey, which found that wartime insistence on military applications of atomic energy had probably held back other developments. This committee had foreseen large power installations and also medical applications of radioactive by-products. A further look at the scientific facts led to the possibility of safer handling:

U-235 and plutonium can be denatured; such denatured materials do not readily lend themselves to the making of atomic explosives, but they can still be used with no essential loss of effectiveness for the peaceful applications of atomic energy.

There is still work to be done on the possibilities of denaturing; research for control and safety is on the list of activities recently recommended by Dr. Oppenheimer to the Atomic Energy Commission of the United Nations. A supplement to the Lilienthal-Acheson report issued by the Department of State, and signed by a group of scientists including Dr. Oppenheimer and Dr. Bacher, warns that "Denaturing, though valuable in adding to the flexibility of a system of controls, cannot of itself eliminate the dangers of atomic warfare." But the report made no such claim.

What the report said was that you could, first, use radioactive materials in scientific or medical work, could go right ahead with that, with no international danger. You could use denatured U-235 or plutonium for "small nuclear reactors" which would make radioactive materials, serving as research tools or subjects for study in physics, chemistry, and biology.

Then, "more marginal from the standpoint of safety, but nevertheless important," would be "high power-level reactors using denatured U-235 and plutonium to develop from 100,000 to 1,000,000 kilowatts of power," in installations without additional uranium or thorium. The committee regards such power reactors as "safe provided there were a minimum of reasonable supervision of their design, construction, and operation." Such presumably is the atomic power station announced for England, to be built at Drigg in Cumberland and to have a production output of 75,000 kilowatts.

The report goes on to say that the material for such installations, opening up atomic power production to private or national enterprise, could not be safely produced except under international control. So the line between safe national or private enterprise, and the ultimate international power, begins to appear. Initial production of fissionable material for power piles is one of the activities to be handled by world co-operative action through what the report calls, tentatively, an "Atomic Development Authority."

Such an Authority would conduct "all the actual mining operations for uranium and thorium." It would, in addition,

. . . own and operate the refineries for the reduction of the ores to the metal or salt. It would own the stockpiles of these

[ 141 ]

materials and it would sell the by-products, such an vanadium and radium. It would also provide the necessary supplies of uranium and thorium for the present limited commercial uses.

All these sales, the report adds, "would presumably go through normal commercial channels."

But the Authority itself would "engage in a wide variety of research activities," including research in atomic explosives, in order to keep ahead of any possible developments which would make its safeguards obsolete. (Somebody out in the woodshed might find out how to make old shoes explode.) On the other hand, there should be a deliberate effort to leave some activities, such as the production of medical aids, to the nations. The Authority would also encourage research—except, of course, research in atomic explosives—by universities, research institutes, and industrial enterprises. Certain other activities—building plants capable of producing fissionable material, or mining uranium—would be, without debate, considered illegal; "the fact that it is the existence of the effort rather than a specific purpose or motive or plan which constitutes an evasion and unmistakable signal" is to be considered an advantage.

The Authority should recruit personnel "on a truly international basis, giving much weight to geographical and national distribution." It would function under the authority of the United Nations, presumably under the Security Council, somewhat as agencies of the United States function under Congress. Aside from United Nations control, there would be an automatic check on the activities of the Authority—somewhat as the Authority would have an automatic check on uranium—in the physical fact that primary power centers could and should be scattered over the world, at localities to be determined not only by strategic balance, but by need for the power developed as a by-product in plants producing stockpiles of fissionable material. Such power could be turned over to the nation or designated user "at the bus bar of the power plant."

Should any impulsive national group try seizure of a power plant or stockpile, it would require a year or so to produce atomic weapons, and the same amount of time would be required to reconvert denatured materials. Thus, the report argues, the surprise element is removed from any possible atomic attack.

The distribution of denatured materials can also be undertaken, it is suggested, without complete disclosure of such details of manufacture as the United States still holds. In this way the transfer of responsibility from the United States to the United Nations can be gradual.

This in brief is the plan which, with a warning about use of the veto power in United Nations action, became the Baruch plan which is still the basis of international debate. Whether or not the veto prohibition is essential to the success of the original committee plan, it is no part of the report; by people as practically minded as the men who wrote the report, the use of a national veto could only be considered like the seizure of a stockpile, advance warning of unfriendly intent. It is not discussed in the report because the political aspects of the transition to international control are not argued.

What is plain to anyone who looks at the report with any knowledge of the Tennessee Valley Authority is that the plan presented by the committee is based on the techniques developed by TVA. The whole approach to the problem, in terms of positive productive action rather than regulation, is the one which worked out in the Tennessee Valley.

There are, of course, certain obvious similarities in the problem. Atomic power is like an unbridled river in that it can destroy; it is also, like river power, capable of constructive use. "The Atomic Development Authority will have the double responsibility of technically effective development, and of safety."

The obstacles to control, again, are not merely physical; they are found chiefly in the established attitudes of political powers. There is also the conflicting or correlative industrial power, with claims and relationships to be considered, and with a strength and influence in most cases exceeding or determining that of the political authorities. There is a necessity, then, to define the powers of a new Authority in terms of a positive usefulness which must make it acceptable to the existing governments. As the report says,

We are satisfied that the differences between national and international operations can be exploited to make the problem of atomic energy manageable. This idea, we think, can become as familiar as the fact that the differences between individual enterprise and corporate enterprise have important consequences in the conduct of business.

Minor problems, too, offer parallels. "How shall nations and individuals be compensated for reserves taken over by the Authority?" asks the report. How were farmers compensated for reservoir land? The committee report does not make recommendations but it says confidently that these things can be managed.

Some of the suggested techniques are obviously recognizable. The Atomic Development Authority is expected to attract good people to work for it, from all over the world—exactly as TVA attracted good people from all over the United States. It should co-operate with universities and research institutes—exactly as TVA co-operated with land-grant colleges and government agencies. The parallels could be extended; it is enough to say that they constitute an important practical recommendation for the plan. The report advances some simple arguments for its recommendations, some rebuttal for anticipated objections:

The program we propose will undoubtedly arouse skepticism when it is first considered. It did among us, but thought and discussion have converted us.

It may seem too idealistic. It seems time we endeavor to bring some of our expressed ideals into being.

It may stem too radical, too advanced, too much beyond human experience. All these terms apply with peculiar fitness to the atomic bomb.

Not merely in the structural resemblance but in the whole spirit of the committee proposal, there is the TVA determination to manage a dangerous waste power for the good of man. There is the intention to do this democratically, sharing the work whenever it can be shared, and enlisting every available agency to help. There is an over-all plan to unite multiple lesser, local activities. There is a promise to find new ways of using the available power. And always there is the weight of TVA experience to show how the thing can be done.

How much of the report, or of the plan, represents the work of David Lilienthal no one can say, not even the members of the committee, who are unanimous in saying that they were unanimous. It is possible to read a sentence here, a paragraph there in the report, which could have been taken from a Lilienthal speech. The directness and simplicity of language is characteristic, and the thought also, as when the possibility of making a seeming difficulty serve the over-all purpose is likened to the wrestler's trick, in jujitsu, that lets the opponent throw himself. David Lilienthal has been doing that all his life.

But members of the committee are emphatic in declaring that they were not dominated or directed by the chairman. They said that eavesdroppers listening, or strangers coming suddenly into a committee session, could not have discovered who the chairman was. One committee member, a top corporation executive, said that at times he wished the chairman would drive a little harder, to get things done faster. Another, a scientist, said that David Lilienthal was a "catalyst," the term used by chemists to describe a substance that causes other substances to react. This same term was used in the early days to describe the effect in the South of the Tennessee Valley Authority.

In a lively account of the committee's experience based

on an interview with Herbert Marks of the State Department,* it was possible to trace Lilienthal's attitude. He had no patience with any proposal to sit still and let nature take its course. "He had a newspaper clipping that he'd wave at us," said Marks. "It was the text of the joint declaration by Attlee, King, and Truman last November in favor of international control. Dave would hold this up in the air and tell us, 'Gentlemen, maybe if you were President of the United States you might have decided differently, but the man who *is* President has committed us to international control, so let's quit considering something our government is opposed to.'"

After insisting that something be done, Lilienthal's great contribution, according to the same story, was helping the committee to relax. He suggested that the duty of drawing up a report be simplified by regarding it as just a letter to a man named Fred. Or five letters, because the members of the committee didn't have to agree. According to one of the consultants quoted in another interview,** it was actually agreed to issue five reports "If any of us felt that the group report lacked directness and honesty." As this committee member explained further, "We were trying to create a collective wisdom." Here, again, the Lilienthal policy of unity through individual independence—or *e pluribus unum*—worked out.

In Mr. Marks' account the sections of the plan suggested by different members of the committee indicate that unity of viewpoint preceded any actual planning. It was

* Daniel Lang in *The New Yorker,* Aug. 17, 1946.
** *Saturday Review of Literature,* June 15, 1946.

not an industrialist, but the scientist, Dr. Oppenheimer, who suggested positive development of atomic energy as an incentive to successful control. It was not the government administrator Lilienthal but the corporation executive Thomas who suggested international control of uranium and thorium mines. It was Lilienthal, in General Groves' plane on the way to Los Alamos, who thought of using the denaturing process to simplify the handling of deadly materials, making it harder to rush into atomic bomb manufacture just as, in prohibition days, it was harder to get drunk on cut whisky.

It was Lilienthal who took the committee home to Norris, and arranged cross-country trips to shake the stiffness out and provide a new perspective.

Because the work of the committee was harmonious as well as efficient, it was natural that when a permanent Atomic Energy Commission was appointed it should be another five-man board, with Lilienthal again its chairman. That he was the proper person for the chairmanship was clear to persons familiar with the report, which, of course, included the scientists who had worked on the Manhattan Project, or who were still working on nuclear research. Opposition to the appointment came from all who had hoped for military control, and who, after losing the Congressional fight against a civilian commission, saw as their next best bet a chairman who would be responsive to military or industrial pressure.

Also, of course, opposition was announced by Senator McKellar of Tennessee, who promised "I will do every-

[ 148 ]

thing in my power to lick him." But if you were in Tennessee at the time the appointment was announced, you knew how to discount the Senator by considering local feeling firsthand. Not that anybody could have foreseen the chorus of praise for David Lilienthal that rose from people and papers that, ten years ago, had fought him tooth and nail. Take the Chattanooga *Times*—a paper famous for its opposition to TVA power during a bond election in the thirties. Said the *Times,* after explaining that it was against Senator McKellar because he was against Lilienthal, "Mr. Lilienthal has already built his monument in enduring stone and in green valleys and a happier and more prosperous people throughout the Tennessee Valley. Few men could wish for a greater career." Maybe it was a little tactless to mention monuments for a man called on to work with bombs, but the friendly intention was clear.

Back in the days of setting up a TVA staff, they used to say that a letter from your home-town preacher was better than any recommendation from a senator. Remembering this, a visitor to the Valley asked a question after Sunday morning service at Norris. "Scotty" Cowan, born a Presbyterian, had long served the international church fellowship at Norris and was, still is, the friend of everybody in the Valley from mill owners to CIO organizers.

"Indeed and I would recommend him," said Mr. Cowan, leaping at the chance. "He has not only the technical ability but the social conscience and the vision needed for the job."

When the appointment was made, David Lilienthal took

the oath in the TVA offices at Knoxville with his hand on a marked copy of the Bible that his mother had given him when he was a boy. He had taken oaths of office before.

"But never before," he said afterward, "did I feel as strongly the force of the words 'So help me God.'"

# IX

*My idea would be not to try logic or reason, but to try to pin the Bolshevik idea on my opponent.*

Testimony of assistant director, Illinois state bureau, National Electric Light Association, in Federal Trade Commission report, 1935.

THE JUNIOR SENATOR from Tennessee, Tom Stewart, has long had one distinction: he was the prosecutor in the Scopes evolution trial. Now the senior senator from Tennessee has stolen his thunder. Seventy-seven-year-old Senator Kenneth McKellar was the self-selected inquisitor of David Lilienthal in the Senate hearings on the Atomic Energy Commission.

At first the Senate conference room where the hearings began escaped the nation-wide interest that focused on the little town of Dayton, Tennessee, in the monkey-trial days. But there were plenty of people to know that in committee hearings, not on the floor, the real work of Congress is done; and in this case drama was promised because the committee to start with seemed fairly evenly divided. Congress had just gone Republican, but the Republicans hadn't had time to make up their minds about atomic energy. While they thought, they saw no harm in

[ 151 ]

letting Senator McKellar question a man whose principal work had been in the South. Though the Senator had just been ousted from presiding over the Senate, he voted Republican as often as most Southern Democrats and had in fact long been supported by the Republicans of East Tennessee.

At the start, Lilienthal ran into a familiar objection: he still looks young for a responsible job, at least young in a group of senators. So they asked him if he realized what an important job it was. He didn't tell them that he had been studying and reporting on atomic energy for over a year; he said

It is difficult to describe one's feeling about the responsibility that this statute rests in the members of the Commission without sounding a little stuffy.

But it is really a terrible responsibility; not only because of the great scope of powers vested, but because errors of judgment, serious errors of judgment, can mean missed opportunity for the people of this country—and even worse.

It was characteristic that he should say "missed opportunity" first, accentuating the positive before he mentioned danger. He had just said, reassuring some senators who had already begun to feel uneasy with a civilian committee in control, that "It ought to be recognized at the outset, without any attempt to pull punches, that atomic energy at the present time, and from the point of view of what seems to me to be the work of the Commission, is essentially a weapon of war." He saw the necessity of military liaison; "However, the statute also has as its objective the development of the peaceful opportunities that are available," and "The important fact to me, and the one that underlies all policy and administration, is this fact: that atomic energy, through most of its course, can be used either for peaceful progress or for destruction."

Some of the senators weren't satisfied with military liaison; they wanted members of the military to sit right with, or on, the Commission all the time. When Lilienthal admitted he hadn't planned that, there was some argument about it, but eventually the senators were persuaded that everything would be all right provided the Commission kept in very close touch, as Lilienthal promised it would, with the Joint Committee.

Lilienthal went further than that. He wanted the people of the country kept notified of the situation too: "This problem of security is going to take an awareness on the part of the American public." He took occasion to mention that maybe the Smyth report had already been a little too revealing about actual processes; what was necessary was to keep people thinking of the implications of the thing, and the necessary policies to be followed:

Really what I think we have got to do is organize a group of from three to five men of great wisdom and understanding and set them to work for this Committee and for the Commission, studying this problem in the light of American customs and ways. We cannot attempt something in the way of security that the American people will not stand for—I mean just ordinary folk.

This reminded the senators of another question; there

[ 153 ]

were those to fear that, having been head of a New Deal agency often described as socialistic, Lilienthal wouldn't give private enterprise its proper share of the atomic energy business. Senator Millikan, recalling that the intention of Congress was to restore controls to private enterprise as soon as consistent with safety and national welfare, asked solemnly: "Are you temperamentally fitted to make that sort of a transition?"

Just as solemnly Mr. Lilienthal said he was. In the Tennessee Valley, he pointed out, they'd done a great deal to help industry, providing it with power and devising new ways for it to make money. With respect to atomic energy, the Commission knew that somehow they must see to it that, to use a colloquialism, "there is something in it for industry."

The committee got more reassurance along this line from one of the other members of the Commission, Rear Admiral Strauss. Mr. Strauss, who explained that he didn't like to be called Admiral, is a Southerner—educated in Virginia—who had worked for Hoover in the food administration days, and had afterward been a partner of Kuhn Loeb & Company, and a director of U. S. Rubber and the Metropolitan Opera. He was definite about the need for the sort of controls which the committee feared:

I consider, Senator, that this force and this art which has been developed is of a nature so remarkable and so revolutionary that it has been found by the Congress not to fit into the scheme of private enterprise to which we have been accustomed and upon which I have been reared. I regard the

[ 154 ]

task of the Atomic Energy Commission as a high public trust: that of being in custodianship of that charge until these problems are resolved to the point where the American pattern can be applied to this subject as well as to any other branch of science or industry.

Mr. Strauss was particularly interested in cancer research; he had lost both parents from the disease and was a trustee of New York's Memorial Hospital. He said of the whole subject of atomic energy:

The importance of it is such to me that I have been willing to sever all my business connections and cut myself off from a substantial income for the purpose of contributing what I may, what I am able, to the work of the Commission.

As a member of the Naval Reserve, formerly of the Army-Navy Munitions Board, Mr. Strauss allayed the Senator's uneasiness about military controls; also, he was reassuringly a banker like Mr. Baruch, whose recommendations they were accustomed to follow.

The next Commissioner to be examined, Sumner T. Pike, represented an opposite but no less successful type of American businessman. A New Englander, educated at Bowdoin and Harvard and now an overseer of Bowdoin, Mr. Pike had gone through a series of miscellaneous jobs from Maine to Texas, to wind up doing well in Wall Street before he became a member of the SEC. He had a Yankee caution about the Commission job; said it was "the only one I ever tackled which seemed further out of reach now than it did the day I looked at it." But he made a good comparison between primitive man's discovery of fire and the discovery of atomic energy. It was very likely, he thought, that man first used fire as a weapon; after he'd chased his neighbor over the hill with a torch, you could see the tribe saying, "Now, this is a pretty good thing. We had better keep it secret."

Just talking to the Commission, who had already had an intensive course on atomic possibilities, was good practice for congressmen who might have lingering delusions about keeping secrets. "The genie is out of the bottle," warned the next member of the Commission, William Wesley Waymack. Mr. Waymack was a newspaper publisher; back in his writing days he'd been a Pulitzer prize winner. He had financial connections too, being a director of the Federal Reserve Bank of Chicago, and he'd got around for the Department of State as an observer in the Greek elections. His paper, though, was in Iowa—the Des Moines *Register*—and Senator Hickenlooper called him Bill.

On the committee of the Carnegie Endowment for International Peace, Mr. Waymack was familiar with the plans for atomic control outlined by that group, which differed from the Baruch proposals chiefly in relying more on national controls. This led into a short discussion of veto power, and Mr. Waymack said that though he'd like to see the bomb pass out of the picture entirely, he didn't want to be in the position of favoring a simple "outlawing" of it as an answer.

"Why not?" asked Senator Bricker, who all along had been for just that. Mr. Waymack explained:

[ 156 ]

Well, I personally think that if we simply make a treaty say-ing that we, the nations signatory to this treaty, agree never to use the atomic bomb in warfare, and stop there—I should not be able, as the years went on, if I lived, to have confidence that nation A, B, X or Y was actually dependable with respect to it. And I assume, while it would not be reasonable to us—I assume the people in nation A, B, X or Y might not have adequate confidence in us.

Questioned earlier, the only scientist member of the Commission, Dr. Robert Fox Bacher, the nuclear physicist, had already contributed his warning about the future. With an impressive university background and partici-pation in practical developments as head of Los Alamos, Dr. Bacher reiterated Lilienthal's assurances of co-oper-ation with the military, complete agreement with the Baruch proposals. But he managed a gentle reminder that time was short:

Whenever I hear statements made by people who say that it will be fifty years before atomic energy is achieved in any usa-ble form, I am always inclined to turn around and look back-ward in time over what has happened in the last four years.

The committee also called Carroll L. Wilson, the Com-mission's general manager. Early in the hearings Lilienthal had taken occasion to speak of the importance of the general manager's job, its equal dignity and prestige since the Commission planned to work together, without sep-arate delegation of duties, as a policy-making body rather than a group of department heads. Mr. Wilson, who had been assistant to Dr. Karl T. Compton at the Massachusetts Institute of Technology, and a special adviser to Dr. Vannevar Bush, had also advised the State Department on atomic energy and had served as secretary of the Lilienthal committee in making its report. Senator Johnson, anxious that the expenses of the whole atomic project be "cut to the bone," asked Mr. Wilson if he had "ever met a pay roll"; fortunately, the reply was yes. Later, Dr. Vannevar Bush was to testify to Mr. Wilson's experience; as executive officer for the Office of Scientific Research and Development, he had been very successful in work parallel to the new management job. Dr. Bush perhaps damaged the effect of this when he admitted that the Office of Scientific Research and Development had spent money freely, considering it secondary to defense and safety; but he was able to say that Mr. Wilson had to his knowledge turned down at least five offers from private business, all better paid than the job as general manager. Later Dr. Karl Compton said one of these jobs would have paid $60,000 a year; so even the senators were impressed.

After the members of the Commission were heard and a few people like Mr. Bernard Baruch and Dr. Conant of Harvard had testified in their favor, the anxieties of the senators had been allayed and it is possible that a vote taken right then would have confirmed the appointments without further argument. But Senator McKellar was there, rarin' to go. He'd already got off to a characteristic start by asking Mr. Lilienthal when he'd first heard about atomic bombs.

"After Hiroshima," the witness answered, like anybody else.

Senator McKellar attached some meaning to this answer that wasn't to be apparent until almost the end of the hearing; at the time, you couldn't tell whether he wanted to prove there had been some sort of leak, or negligence on the part of Mr. Lilienthal in not finding out more. He went on; didn't Mr. Lilienthal know that hundreds of years ago Macedonian scientists, under Alexander the Great, had tried to split the atom?

If you knew Southern politicians you could understand this as an attempt to show off, but the chairman had to ask for quiet. That research for Alexander was to come up again and again, until newspaper men at the hearings formed an Association of Macedonian Scientists. Witnesses were polite; the only one to express even a slight dissent from the Senator's history was Dr. Conant, who said mildly, "I wouldn't want to challenge you, but it would be news to me."

Examining Lilienthal, McKellar went on to ask how it was that a man who hadn't known about the bomb was to be placed at the head of this great project, when the man who discovered the bomb had been relieved of responsibility. By discoverer it developed that the Senator meant General Groves, Army head of the Manhattan Project; and McKellar was only dramatizing his opposition to the civilian commission, his preference for leaving the whole business in the hands of the military.

Naturally this was a criticism of Congress, not of the

[ 159 ]

witness. But Senator McKellar was to prove he had many lines of attack.

McKellar: Mr. Lilienthal, I wanted to ask you about another thing. Were your father and mother born in Illinois?

Lilienthal: No, they were not. They were born in Austria-Hungary.

McKellar: What place in Austria-Hungary?

Lilienthal: I confess I do not know the name, but I will supply that.

McKellar: Now, there are some other things that I want to ask you about. Are you a Communist?

Lilienthal: No.

McKellar: Are you a Democrat?

Lilienthal: No.

McKellar: Are you a Republican?

Lilienthal: No. I am like a great many other people, not affiliated with any political party. I am an independent voter.

The next day, Mr. Lilienthal was able to report that his parents were born in a village "in the vicinity of Pressburg, which is now a part of Czechoslovakia."

McKellar: Which is now a part of Czechoslovakia. And as a matter of fact, Czechoslovakia is under the domination of Russia, is it not?

Lilienthal: That is a complicated question. I wouldn't know.

McKellar: Well, if you don't want to answer it, it is your privilege not to do it.

Lilienthal: My father and mother were born in that area quite a long time ago. My father is 78 years old and my

[ 160 ]

mother is 72. And I am sure that you are giving them very great pain by the maltreatment that you are giving me in these hearings, Senator.

Unabashed, the Senator moved into the field of his real interest. For fourteen long years, McKellar had been bitterly disappointed in TVA on two counts: its employment policy had afforded no toehold for Congressional patronage, and the act giving the Authority the flexibility of a corporation had permitted the use of funds without previous clearance through the Appropriations Committee. Senator McKellar is chairman of that committee.

Regarding TVA employment policies, Lilienthal had already refused to bite. "Senator, ever since we had our first meeting on this subject, in 1933, we have understood each other very well." But the Senator tried the appropriations issue:

McKellar: Will you have to pay your profits on atomic energy into the Treasury of the United States, or will you take the same position about the profits from atomic energy that you took with respect to the profits from the several dams that were built down in the Tennessee Valley?

Lilienthal: I will do as I did in the case of the TVA: follow the terms of the law.

Now in trying to make ridiculous or objectionable TVA's plowing of "profits" back into the land, McKellar established Lilienthal's point that the Authority had been a useful stimulus to business. Was it true, asked the Senator, that TVA had been interested in a laminated lumber

[ 161 ]

plant? In a quick-freezing plant? In portable threshers? Had they fooled around with strawberry-capping machines and ham-curing devices?

"On an experimental and noncommercial basis, yes," Lilienthal admitted. More, the experiments "have formed the basis of successful private businesses, which are taken very seriously by men in the Tennessee Valley who are in them."

But hadn't TVA competed with private business? If the Senator meant the 138 municipal districts in which TVA power was used, said Lilienthal, there was no longer any competition, because the utilities had sold out. No, but how about fertilizer? Lilienthal explained that during the recent war, Muscle Shoals nitrates had no longer been needed for explosives so the plant had been turned back to its original Wilsonian purpose, the wartime production of nitrate fertilizer, of which there was a shortage.

The Senator went off on another track; hadn't the government lost money on Muscle Shoals? Lilienthal hadn't in his head the figures asked for; that, he said, was what books were for, and assistants, and at that point he made an engaging confession:

I want to warn the Senate that they had better not confirm me if it is their expectation that I carry a great miscellany of figures in my head. I just don't operate that way and that may be a major handicap, in which case you ought to know about it.

Direct connection with Russia being difficult to prove—

McKellar had asked if Lilienthal had been there, and the answer was no—he moved into the field of ideas. He asked once too often if Lilienthal wasn't communistic in his sympathies. He got an answer:

This I do carry in my head, Senator. I will do my best to make it clear. My convictions are not so much concerned with what I am against as what I am for; and that excludes a lot of things automatically.

Traditionally, democracy has been an affirmative doctrine rather than merely a negative one.

I believe—and I so conceive the Constitution of the United States to rest, as does religion upon—the fundamental proposition of the integrity of the individual; and that all Government and all private institutions must be designed to promote and protect and defend the integrity and the dignity of the individual; that that is the essential meaning of the Constitution and the Bill of Rights, as it is essentially the meaning of religion.

Any form of government, therefore, and any other institutions which make men means rather than ends in themselves, which exalt the state or any other institutions above the importance of men, which place arbitrary power over men as a fundamental tenet of government, are contrary to this conception; and therefore I am deeply opposed to them.

The Communistic philosophy as well as the Communistic form of government fall within this category, for their fundamental tenet is quite to the contrary. The fundamental tenet of Communism is that the state is an end in itself, and that therefore the powers which the state exercise over the individual are without any ethical standards to limit them.

That I deeply disbelieve.

[ 163 ]

It is very easy simply to say one is not a Communist. And of course if despite my record it is necessary for me to state that very affirmatively, then it is a great disappointment to me. It is very easy to talk about being against communism. It is equally important to believe those things which provide a satisfactory and effective alternative. Democracy is that satisfying affirmative alternative.

Its hope in the world that it is an affirmative belief, rather than being simply a belief against something else and nothing more.

One of the tenets of democracy that grow out of this central core of a belief that the individual comes first, that all men are the children of God and their personalities are therefore sacred, is a great belief in civil liberties and their protection, and a repugnance to anyone who would steal from a human being that which is most precious to him, his good name; by impugning things to him, by innuendo or by insinuations. And it is especially an unhappy circumstance that occasionally that is done in the name of democracy. This I think is something that can tear our country apart and destroy it—if we carry it further.

I deeply believe in the capacity of democracy to surmount any trials that may lie ahead, provided only we practice it in our daily lives. And among the things we must practice is this: that while we seek fervently to ferret out the subversive and anti-democratic forces in the country, we do not at the same time, by hysteria, by resort to innuendo, and sneers, and other unfortunate tactics, besmirch the very cause that we believe in, and cause a separation among our people, cause one group and one individual to hate another, based on mere attacks, mere unsubstantiated attacks upon their loyalty.

I want also to add that part of my conviction is based on

[ 164 ]

my training as an Anglo-American common lawyer. It is the very basis and the great heritage of the English people to this country which we have maintained, that the strictest rules of credibility of witnesses be maintained, and hearsay and the gossip shall be excluded in courts of justice. And that, too, is an essential of our democracy.

And whether by administrative agencies acting arbitrarily against business organizations, or whether by investigating activities of the legislative branches, whenever those principles of the protection of an individual and his good name against besmirchment by gossip, hearsay and the statements of witnesses who are not subject to cross-examination then, too, we have failed in carrying forward our ideals in respect to democracy. This I deeply believe. . . .

When Mr. Lilienthal finished trying to make it clear, there was a little silence. Then Senator McMahon said, "I congratulate you on that statement. In my opinion it is the creed of a very real American."

As far as appointment confirmation went, the matter was definitely decided that day, or certainly by the time the next day's papers came out. The Lilienthal "credo," as it came to be called, appeared on front pages all over the country, and formed the text of countless editorials. As soon as schedules permitted it was reprinted in magazines as diverse as *Life* and the *New Republic*. It was recommended for inclusion in literary anthologies, and for reading in the schools. It was compared to the Gettysburg Address and to the Declaration; it was mentioned in the same breath with the Ten Commandments and the Golden Rule.

Spontaneously though deliberately spoken, not read, it was remarkable on that account, although anybody as smart as David Lilienthal of course knew that McKellar's nagging would afford plenty of opportunity for such a statement. The timing was important, and the delivery, although it was interesting to notice that the reporters writing about it afterward disagreed as to just how the words were said. Some said Lilienthal looked hard at McKellar, others that he turned to face the committee— the truth, of course, being that in the course of a fairly long speech he did both.

The real question was how the speaker came to think the way he did. This interested Lilienthal himself, when he found that he had touched off such a burst of approval, saying what so many people thought should be said. And he found, what anybody would know, that the basic ideas had been in his mind a long time. Hunting through old papers to find some school pictures—Mrs. Lilienthal is a keeper of mementos and clippings, as the wife of a man in public life should be—the family found a copy of a speech that David Eli Lilienthal, aged eighteen, had made in a state oratorical contest in Indiana during the first World War. Better than anything else could, that speech tells you what the boy David was like, and—allowing for seasoning, a lightening of the tragic note that living teaches you to lighten, but with a firm hold on the same principles—it shows what the man is like today.

Some men, arriving where David Lilienthal now is, would pass over the eighteen-year-old's frank avowal of what some people would consider a handicap. Lilienthal looks, acts, and most of the time seems to think like a plain Hoosier, and of course you can't tell from his name; after he was head of TVA, an indignant correspondent from Brooklyn wrote to reprove a reporter: "You are evidently under the impression that he is of Jewish ancestry. If you will make inquiry, you will find that he and his forebears are and have been Lutherans and that he is also what Hitler would call pure Aryan." Just by saying nothing, Lilienthal could let a lot of people go on thinking that. In a way it would be fair because he isn't held down by any narrow creed; one Southerner, discovering the South, noticed that you could have bacon for breakfast on the Lilienthal terrace at Norris.

But David Lilienthal isn't forgetting how he learned that part of his "credo" about the brotherhood of man under the fatherhood of God. He gave a copy of the school oration to a little religious magazine, and he's right to want people to read it.

You can see an eighteen-year-old boy making that speech, standing tense but trying to relax the way the teachers had told him to, while he went back in history as good students do, to talk about the past of the Jewish people:

Singing in the midnight watches of Egyptian bondage, building cities to the pride of hated kings, standing "amid the ruins of the last dark hour of national life"; enduring the horrors of the Spanish Inquisition; lifting his low moaning amid the bloody scourgings of Germany; cringing through the centuries before the anathemas of Italy, France and England; patiently accumulating wealth for the plunder of the Russian; through all the burnings at the stake, the crucifixions, the tortures inflicted even in the name of Christ—through the bleak tragedy making bloody all the years, the Jew has remained, the paradox of the world.

This was spoken during the first World War, but some of the things the speaker said would be true when the wheel swung full circle for the second:

Thus runs the tragic, persistent story of the Jew. But what of him today, when the drunken earth lifts to heaven the scream of charging soldiery, mingling with the wail of starving women and children?

Through all time the paragon of sufferers, he is today one of the most pitiful victims of all this orgy of blood. A citizen of every belligerent nation, he is in the army of every country now at war. The Jew presents the anomaly of a nationality arrayed against itself—of blood fighting blood. The Austrian Jew fires across "No Man's Land" into the heart of a brother Italian Jew; the German Jew must starve the wife and children of a Belgian Jew. Every gory charge is against his own. Every day runs livid with accounts of the massacre of Russian Jews in counterrevolutions; of their starvation in pillaged Poland; their shameless slaughter in the streets of Jerusalem by the besieged Turk.

And the young man would have lifted his head, but not his voice, as he said:

The telling of this tragedy is bitterness unspeakable, for I am a Jew! The anguish of my people is my anguish; the immortal yearning of my people, thank God, is mine too.

On the bright side he went on to talk about "the unconquerable faith of the Jew":

Still today clearly and distinctly shine the Ten Commandments of the Jew Moses; a million tongues daily extol the Almighty through the songs of Israel's psalmist, David; and a fifth of the people of the world prayerfully beseech the blessing of God in the name of a Galilean prophet, Jesus the Jew!

But no young man of eighteen would want to stop with past achievements; he'd want to think of the future. This particular David looked for "a rational statement as to the ultimate mission of the Jew," and found it was this mission "to help establish among men, as the inexorable principle of all life, the law of unity. The mission of the Jew is to teach the reunion, the refraternization, and internationalization of mankind; to make all men feel that they are one, that they have one loving Father."

Facing what looked like a difficulty, he went on to ask how this could be accomplished by a people scattered, subject, without a country; and, as he was to do later in life, he turned the difficulty to advantage: "This despised people can hasten world harmony because of their unified dispersion. His physical and spiritual home destroyed, the Jew, embodying the message of unity, went forth, the Messiah of nations. . . . He is a universal citizen, a potential world patriot."

Because unity was the major tenet of his religion, there-

[ 169 ]

fore of his life, the speaker said, the Jew must help establish enduring harmony. It was this young man who was to unify a river region, with a "multipurpose program" that was a sort of unified dispersion of benefits to people in a country where he'd come as a stranger; it was the same young man who was to find even bigger need to be a universal citizen and a world patriot. And in the battle this brought on he was to find his best defense in a simple restatement of words said thirty years before—that in the unity of God, the basic principle of Jewish religion, "We find also the dominating idea of the unity of man, of his common brotherhood and common fatherhood, the true basis of democracy."

Down in the Valley where they know David Lilienthal best, they wouldn't associate that young speech with him as far as its emotional language goes, or its speaking out for the Jews, because they know Mr. Lilienthal as a calm, good-natured man, like anybody else except maybe smarter. They don't think of him as Jewish or as in any way concerned with a Jewish problem; of course they haven't got that problem, as they will tell you, down there.

As for being a Communist, or favoring Communism in TVA, anybody living in the Valley would laugh, now, at that. They wouldn't need a speech from David Lilienthal to know he was a man with the fear of God in him, which Communists, they know, do not have. They wouldn't need a speech, or two speeches, to know that all his life, man and boy, he'd believed in democracy and practiced it.

But they know how easy it is for people to get mixed up about names. Over at Tellico Plains in Tennessee, up in the neighborhood of Hiwassee dam, there are animals called, locally, Russian hogs. These Russian hogs aren't like ordinary hogs—they are fighting animals, running wild in the woods; so every year or so they organize a hunt and go out and deal with them. If you talk about Russian hogs, most people around Tellico Plains know what you mean, but smart people there, including some of the TVA men, know they aren't Russian hogs at all. They are Prussian boars, brought to the Smokies years ago by an Englishman who liked to stick pig.

As for the religion in the speech, it's like young David said. Good people can stand together on it, in the Valley or in the world.

X

*We cannot live without war. Should we make peace with
the Tuscaroras, we must immediately look out for some
other with whom we can engage in our beloved occupation.*

Cherokee chief, quoted
by G. P. THURSTON in
*Antiquities of Tennessee.*

THE "I BELIEVE" SPEECH is a splendid example of the characteristic Lilienthal method: state your position in terms
of affirmative good rather than negative ill, and act accordingly. But in dealing with McKellar it is never possible to
stop with a positive truth, since the opposite statement is
certain to be made. That day in the committee room the
Senator proceeded quite as if Lilienthal had not spoken;
he reverted to Russia and supplied a little comedy relief
by going into the TVA provision, under Lend-Lease, of
plans for dams to be built in the Soviet Union. In thus
helping Russia, the Senator asked, making it sound like a
personal whim, had Mr. Lilienthal had any correspondence
with Commissar Stalin? Commissar Molotov? No, the witness explained, he wasn't in that class. The Senator tried
a few less famous names, to which Lilienthal not only said
no but added sympathetically that the consonants were
"hard on the dentures, Senator." McKellar asked if he

[ 172 ]

hadn't had a letter of thanks from the Russians, after helping them. No?

McKellar: As a matter of fact, you feel exceedingly friendly to Russia, do you not?

Lilienthal: I have the greatest sympathy for the Russian people, and not in order to be confirmed to this post or any other would I utter irresponsible expressions of hatred against the people of Russia.

He added that he thought people under a totalitarian state were misled, but McKellar had skipped back to this country with the mention of a Dies Committee rumor that there were fifty-five Communist sympathizers in TVA. Actually the Dies investigator had reported a total of fifty-five in the Knoxville area, which was something quite different; the party organizer's boast of TVA employees so inclined was seven, out of some 18,200. But throughout the hearings McKellar stuck to his fifty-five Communists "right under your nose in TVA—you didn't know? You never made any effort to rid TVA of these Communists?"

This brought from Lilienthal a speech that in some ways was more important to American liberty than his "credo":

No. Let me explain why.

To explain why, one must describe the procedure of the Dies Committee on Un-American Activities.

The procedure was this: Citizens, people generally, would write in to the Dies Committee and report their suspicions about subversive activities they believed were going on, or individuals whom they suspected of being guilty of subversive

[ 173 ]

activities or belonging to the Communist Party, and so on. There was no responsibility attached to such charges. And it was a matter of common knowledge that some of these reports were presented by people with the best of motives but with poor judgment. Some were presented by people who had evidence, and some on the basis of malice.

They were submitted by jilted suitors and disgruntled employees, and a great variety of people; or by people who themselves had been accused of communism and sought to drag in someone else by saying that they had associated with him.

This is the typical mass of gossip and innuendo and suspicion—mixed with fact—that experienced investigators are familiar with, and that is the basis of many of the protections of civil rights under our form of the common law.

These reports were then sifted, and a good many of them were thrown out completely, because they were obviously without any basis at all.

Others were reexamined, and investigators sent out. And others were pursued in a different way. Then a hearing was had. In the case of the TVA, there was a hearing before the commissioner himself, Mr. Joe Starnes. And he took testimony, and he discarded those accusations that were obviously without any basis.

The point that I am making is that it was well known that mere accusation of communism or Communist learnings in itself, without further support, could not be considered a matter for concern by an Administrator.

To do otherwise, Lilienthal said parenthetically, would be to participate in the witch-hunting which, in one form or another, had persisted for long periods of human history. "There are always witch-hunters, and people who will gladly defame and assassinate the character of others, without responsibility. That is why we have a system of laws, and that is why we have courts, and that is why we have rules of evidence."

It was only after a report from the Dies Committee, Lilienthal went on to explain, that appropriate administrative action could be taken:

That was the course pursued. Mr. Starnes sent his analysis of this hearing to the board, and on that basis administrative action was taken.


McKellar: Did you keep a record—

Lilienthal: May I complete this statement? It is fairly important, and will become increasingly important if this sort of character assassination becomes a national habit, which I deeply hope it will not.

It is important to bear in mind that there was no responsibility at all attached to a man who pointed his finger at his neighbor and said "I believe he is a Communist," or "I believe he was seen some place with somebody who once was seen with Communists."

There will be no protection at all for the good name of any citizen of this country if we don't go back to the fundamental principles of the Bill of Rights and the common law in the sifting of evidence. And I feel strongly about that.

I am quite ready to be lynched if, in the process of that lynching, this lesson about what our history means is learned —and what the history of the common law means in terms of the protection of the individual against irresponsible charges of witch-hunters.

[ 175 ]

McKellar of course had the trial lawyer's ability to ignore a squelching. He reverted to his last question:

McKellar: Mr. Lilienthal, did you not keep a record of these legal hearings that you had?

Lilienthal: I haven't made myself clear. There were no hearings before the Board. The hearings were before Mr. Starnes, who is a legislator and the vice-chairman of the Dies Committee.

McKellar: I thought you said when these boys were charged you gave them hearings there in your Commission.

Lilienthal: No.

McKellar: You did not give them any hearings in your Commission?

Lilienthal: No, it wasn't necessary to, because the Dies Committee themselves threw these things out as having no value.

That charges should have been considered baseless by the Dies Committee was the ultimate in negation, but this irony was lost on Senator McKellar. Of the definition of democracy in the "credo" he said reproachfully, "The other day when I asked you if you were a Democrat, you said you were not." He went on:

McKellar: You said democracy is a belief in man's dignity. I want to know what you mean.

Lilienthal: Do you really, Senator?

McKellar: Yes, sir, I want to know what you mean.

Lilienthal: I have no desire to be offensive to the Senator, but among other things that I had in mind was what seemed to me the clear tendency of the senior Senator from Tennessee in making accusations—a tendency which seems to me not in the best tradition of democratic institutions: in the course of a proceeding of this kind, to make charges of communism or subversive beliefs against people who are not present, or people who being present do not have the protection of counsel, who do not have the right of cross-examination, and do not have any of the protections that for many centuries have been regarded as an essential part of the rights protecting the individual.

Undeterred by these remarks, Senator McKellar proceeded to read aloud one of the more obviously erroneous lists of TVA employees accused of leftist leanings, and to repeat his Communist-meeting charge. This drew a further response from Lilienthal:

The Senator asked me a little while ago what I meant by the hazards in abandoning the traditional safeguards of the rights of individuals, among which perhaps the greatest is the right to his good name and the right not to be besmirched by statements that are not verified.

And I may say that there are many historical precedents for that very thing—from the days of Salem withcraft, the alien and sedition laws, and other landmarks of history—for the process in which the Senator is now indulging, if I may say so without any disrespect at all.

These are the unsubstantiated statements of people whose credibility has not been established against people who are not here to defend themselves. . . . These are not fair procedures. That is what I was talking about, Senator.

Let me say this further: that the Dies committee itself recognized this and did have a hearing. It was not a judicial hearing, but it was a hearing before men of some legal background and training and understanding of these matters.

What Lilienthal could not say was that the smear technique does not require that charges be established, but only that they be made. This fact McKellar continued to demonstrate. And while his subpoenas followed up seven-year-old rumors which had proved inadequate even for Dies, he found another source of unsupported charges by going a little farther back. He summoned Dr. Arthur Morgan from the quiet of Yellow Springs, Ohio, where since leaving TVA the former chairman had been congenially engaged in writing a life of Edward Bellamy. Dr. Morgan had no wish to look backward at the TVA experience, but on demand he repeated many of the things he had said in 1938. He still felt suspicious of David Lilienthal, still felt he had "contrary purposes," and he was still conscious of his own rightful position as chairman of the board. He was suspicious, too, of Francis Biddle, and still unsuspicious of power-company propaganda. On the other hand, to McKellar's disappointment he was still painfully honest. Asked whether, having suggested the appointment of two other members of a five-man commission, Lilienthal would therefore try to control their votes, Dr. Morgan said not necessarily. Dr. Morgan went farther, to boost TVA by saying that since he had left, a good many of his recommendations had been carried out.

Senator McKellar was too smart to ask Dr. Morgan about the people he hoped to prove were Communists in TVA, because these were people going back to Dr. Arthur's own

[ 178 ]

day as chairman. The original Dies investigation had turned up a feud waged by a man who lost his TVA job, and who felt there had been a Communist conspiracy against him. This was in the days when, in the South, the words Communist and CIO were considered interchangeable. The ex-employee had been considered a bad supervisor because he was shocked and disgusted when the file clerks in his department voted to change their union affiliation from AFGE, the AFL union, to UFW, CIO. Although his case was carried through the elaborate system of hearings developed by TVA personnel, he felt himself the victim of TVA lawyers, one of whom had shown support for another CIO union, the Newspaper Guild. To make it worse, this lawyer was named Marks.

Another disgruntled former employee had been let out of TVA's legal department, and without putting it just that way, he contributed the fact that there were at one time three Jewish lawyers working for the Authority, not counting Lilienthal. As proof of conspiracy he submitted the sinister suggestion that these men called each other by their first names, and although Lilienthal denied personal acquaintance with one of the men mentioned, he had to admit that "Everybody calls me Dave."

The TVA lawyer named Marks had been named counsel for the Atomic Energy Commission, and it required testimony from Donald Nelson, Dean Acheson of the State Department, John Lord O'Brian, and the president of Dartmouth College to allay Senator McKellar's alarm. It developed that Herbert Marks was known to a good many people, some of them not even New Dealers, for his work on power allocations during the war. As the Secretary of the Interior said, "If Herb Marks is a Communist, so is Bob Taft."

While the Communist issue hung fire, McKellar offered other evidence; a Nashville banker who didn't like TVA said so, and a man in Wisconsin who hadn't approved of Lilienthal as utilities commissioner wrote to accuse him of "red leanings." Also, hopefully publicized by the Hearst papers, a girl from Chicago who had been Lilienthal's secretary came to say he had kept an office there, finishing up the editing job for Public Utilities and Carriers Service, after he had gone to work in Wisconsin. As the Wisconsin law provided that the utilities commissioner should hold no other job, it took a telegram from Philip La Follette to explain that he knew all about Lilienthal's windup of the Chicago business, it was all right, and he hoped the Senate committee would get on with its job of confirmation.

Meanwhile other people took the stand as witnesses to say the same thing. Dr. Vannevar Bush said he had known Mr. Lilienthal about fifteen years; "I regard him as a great American, and I am proud that he is my friend." Dr. Karl Compton said that Lilienthal's name was "on every list I saw" for the Commission. Bishop E. E. Hughes of the Methodist Church, past president and trustee of DePauw, told the Committee that the clergy of eighteen states wanted the Commission confirmed. He added that Lilienthal's ability and character had been recognized in the days when they made him president of the student body at DePauw. He confessed that even ministers could be accused of Communist sympathies. "This," he explained to the senators, "is not so much because the accusers are bad or mean as because they are plain scared. But our chief fright, gentlemen, should be about the atomic bomb itself."

Actually it wasn't clear that fright was the basis of the charge of Communism directed at people working for TVA back in 1940. Spite could have had something to do with it. Dies Committee investigations had turned up one young employee who honestly admitted that at the age of nineteen, and while employed by TVA, he had joined the Communist party. Only two other persons working for TVA were admitted party members, but a letter supposedly signed by the young enthusiast, Henry C. Hart, and addressed to a party organizer, mentioned other names. The letter also told with glee about the Communist conspiracy against the chief of the files, Mr. Smith, who had lost his job after objecting to the CIO union.

This letter had not been used in the Dies Committee hearings but it was published in the Knoxville *Journal,* and the *Journal* had used a mimeographed copy from the Dies office. Senator McKellar read and reread the letter into the record, but was unable to produce either the original or a photostat. Two people were competent witnesses: Congressman Joe Starnes, who had held the Dies hearings, and Mr. Hart, who had testified at those hearings but had not been asked about the letter. At Lilienthal's request Mr. Starnes was called as a witness, and Senator McKellar could hardly wait for a chance to question Mr. Hart.

While he waited, another witness served to remind any forgetful reporters of what the Dies hearings had been like.

[ 181 ]

She introduced herself as Mrs. Agnes Waters, 3267 N Street, N.W., Washington, and she objected first of all, quoting George Washington, to the appointment of a civilian commission. Further:

I am here to protest against the nomination of Mr. David Lilienthal and of Mr. Lewis Lichenstein Strauss, an international banker and member of the Kuhn Loeb & Company firm.

These men are suspicious characters, and I am protesting against their appointment. . . .

I consider their appointment to the Atomic Commission, and this civilian Atomic Commission itself the greatest tragedy, the gravest betrayal of mankind, and the most awful blunder since the crucifixion of our Lord Jesus Christ, and it is part of a conspiracy for world government by the international bankers.

And while there has been some allusion to Mr. Lilienthal's activities as a Communist, I think he is merely a small stooge alongside of the men that are behind this Atomic Energy Commission.

Mr. Barney Baruch, Mr. Lewis Strauss and Mr. Jacob Schiff of Kuhn Loeb & Company were the men who financed the revolution in Russia. I have the evidence with me today to give to you.

At this point Senator Hickenlooper interrupted. "May I suggest, Madam, that you are making some rather strong statements?"

The lady continued confident. "Oh, I can substantiate

anything I have stated." She went back to the error of a civilian commission:

It is a direct violation of these protective laws assuring our national defense that civilian commissioners are appointed, especially of subversive elements. Why, to think that even a scintilla of suspicion should accrue to a man charged with the power of the Atomic Energy Commission.

And I know I can point out to you two on that commission that I would say were enemies of this Republic. And that the most important and diabolical weapon of modern warfare should be bandied about . . . taken from the guardianship of our U. S. Army officials who have taken an oath to give their lives in defense of this Republic . . . to be bandied about and exposed to our enemies within our gates, and is now to be placed by the Congress of the United States in the hands of men whose integrity is in doubt.

Now, Mr. Barney Baruch—

Again the chairman interrupted. "I may say at this point, Madam, that I feel that it is the universal opinion of every member of this Committee that there can be no possible question cast at the personal integrity of any appointee."

Mrs. Waters stopped only to rebuke him.

Well, that is a pitiful statement for you to make, you who have been elected by the people to protect the rights of the people, and when you can smell this rat a mile off, and you know it. . . .

[ 183 ]

Maybe you are an ignoramus. Maybe you don't know what you are talking about. . . .

That is the sort of statement where people have all their votes in the bag beforehand, where we were sold down the river to these New Dealers in the first and second World Wars, with Mr. Barney Baruch with his fingers dipping in blood— dipping in the blood of every family from London to Timbuktu. . . .

The evidence referred to by the witness turned out to be a photostat of a New York *Times* story of a meeting in New York to celebrate the downfall of the Czars. In some way she connected this with "Admiral Strauss, wrapping himself up in the American flag and coming here to take the atomic bomb and build a world government for Russia. And I charge him with it." More,

Mr. Jacob A. Schiff was the former president of Kuhn Loeb & Company. And this gentleman is praised, and says he is beyond the reach of poor dear old Senator McKellar who is making a brave effort to defend America.

It was, Mrs. Waters continued, the international bankers who "have ripped the world down to build a Jewish dynasty. And it is a very suspicious circumstance that only Jews have been appointed recently by the President of the United States. This is a Christian country, a great Christian nation, and this is a Christian world, and we intend to maintain it, too. The Church of Christ is not going down as it went down in Russia and in all those countries of Europe."

At this point Senator McMahon suggested that this was going beyond the pale.

"I haven't gone beyond the pale. These men are allowed days and hours of time. You are not going to restrict me. No, sir."

"Do you have any proof?"

The witness flourished the story about the friends of Russian freedom in 1917, then went back to the Russo-Japanese war of 1902. "Now, this is vital to all of you and I wish you would maintain order for me." She appealed to the chair: "Will you get order back in here? These Jews are whispering."

Said the chairman: "Madam, you asked for fifteen minutes. Your fifteen minutes has expired."

To anyone who followed the Dies testimony or heard broadcasts beamed at this country from Nazi Berlin, this sort of thing is familiar, but it was a great relief to hear former Congressman Joe Starnes of Alabama, next to Martin Dies the most earnest member of the original committee, who came soon after. Summoned to talk about the Dies investigation of TVA, Mr. Starnes began by commending David Lilienthal as "A man of impeccable character. I have never heard aught against the personal life and character of Mr. Lilienthal." More, "as a public official I regard him as an able administrator, a good executive, conscientious in the performance of his duties, and a man with vision and character, energy and realism."

Mr. Starnes explained that he had been on the Appropriations Committee of the House, as well as on the Dies

Committee, so had an opportunity to know the TVA chairman in a business way:

We in the Valley have a very high regard for him as a man and as a Government official.

I have heard him talk to groups of farmers, to laborers, to business men and professional men throughout the Valley many times. . . . I followed the course of all the investigations. As you know, the TVA was investigated by a joint congressional committee, thoroughly and searchingly. . . . It had to run the gamut of all the Federal Courts, including the Supreme Court, and was subjected to legal attack by the very best legal brains that could be procured in this country. . . .

Mr. Lilienthal's appointment, I think, was an exceedingly fine appointment on the part of the President. Mr. Lilienthal has operated in a new field before and has done the job well.

Mr. Starnes continued to say truthfully that the atomic energy job required "somebody who has vision, who has idealism, and who also has some practical common sense; one who is not afraid to take a subject that is new under the sun and chart a course for the benefit of humanity." Going "from the regional and national to the international field," he thought the Committee "fortunate to have a man of his background and experience."

Coming to the Communist issue, Mr. Starnes made a claim which was, to anyone familiar with the Dies record, an understatement. "I know of no one on the face of the earth that would question my hostility to Communism. Under no stretch of imagination could I be accused of looking with the slightest degree of favor upon Com-

[ 186 ]

munism or statism in any form." With this prelude, Mr. Starnes launched upon an explanation of Knoxville in 1940.

There had been a taxicab strike down there, which brought down some New York Communists. At the same time, the TVA white-collar union had changed over to CIO. There were disgruntled people fired from TVA, or dissatisfied over the union business, who made charges; there was much hearsay testimony, no evidence except for the most gullible.

People had meetings, for the CIO or Spanish war aid, but they weren't Communist meetings. Some of the people accused were WPA workers, not TVA workers. The Authority's handling of the three party members uncovered was "entirely satisfactory" to the Dies Committee. Mr. Starnes concluded:

Now, let me say this: with all the emphasis at my command, I want to say that at no time during the course of this investigation was there a charge that Mr. Lilienthal was a member of the Communist Party, had participated in its activities or was sympathetic to its program.

The same can be said of Mr. Clapp, of Mr. Swidler, and every other man in a high responsible administrative or policy-making position.

I don't know of anything else I could say, Mr. Chairman.

Senator McKellar thought of a few things. Of course Mr. Starnes knew that Communists always denied being Communists? And what about the Hart letter? The letter, said Mr. Starnes, was not in the Dies files, nor a photostat of it, at the time of his investigation. There were only "mimeographed sheets of what purported to be a letter." Nevertheless—

McKellar: Do you not think, Mr. Starnes, that in the present condition of the world, and especially in the present condition of ourselves, with the empire or dynasty or whatever it may be called of Russia, and after thinking of the wonderful discovery that was made by the government under General Groves, the atomic discovery, do you not think that we ought to be exceedingly careful of the people whom we put on the Board? Would you not want people that were just known by the world to be absolutely . . .
Starnes: Like Caesar's wife, above suspicion?
McKellar: Your illustration is good.
Starnes: I certainly would, sir.

Two Southerners together, the former congressman and the senator then indulged in a little reminiscence. Mr. Starnes had been in the war, with SHAEF and with the military government of Berlin, the Potsdam conference. . . .

"All that convinces me that here at home the greatest threat to our institutions and to us as a people—as a free people—comes to us from the insidious activities of the Communist party."

Senator McKellar said he agreed a thousand per cent.

"Working," Mr. Starnes continued an old speech, "through the medium of labor unions, of schools and colleges, and of whatever means are available to them to control the sources of information in this country."

[ 188 ]

As they swapped compliments, the senator at last relieved the itch that had pestered him since the start of the hearings, and his questions about Hiroshima were explained. He got it into the record that, in return for helping pass the $2,600,000,000 appropriation, he had been told by the War Department when the planes took off, *before* Hiroshima was hit.

You could of course say that Mr. Starnes was not a disinterested witness because he came from Guntersville, where TVA built a dam, but otherwise you couldn't ask for any more telling testimony to settle a Communism charge. Senator McKellar, however, persisted. To establish the Hart letter he brought a policeman from Birmingham, Alabama, who told how he had arrested a man he thought was a Communist—you could, he said in response to inquiry, do that in Alabama—and used his keys to open the files at Communist headquarters. With him had been a Dies investigator named Barker, and they had taken this letter out and had it photostated. He couldn't remember where.

"Unless some substantial proof of the genuineness of the letter is produced I shall wholly discount it in my mind," said Chairman Hickenlooper.

But Senator McKellar wasn't going to let a witness brought clear from Birmingham go to waste. "Do you," he asked, "believe it would be wise to appoint as the head of the Atomic Energy Commission, the greatest disturber in the world and the greatest destroyer of mankind, probably, in the world, anyone but a thousand per cent American?"

"Absolutely not," said the Birmingham policeman.

[ 189 ]

The Senator also brought as a witness the Dies Committee investigator, Barker, who told a fascinating spy story and suggested that maybe they hadn't used the letter because it had been seized illegally. Just about that time, he recalled, there had been some trouble in the courts about illegal seizures up in Philadelphia. "And he sends old Barker down to Birmingham and he comes back with a dead cat—another piece of evidence that has been seized illegally." But he hadn't shown the letter or the Dies file on TVA to the Knoxville *Journal:* he was sure of that. "There wasn't a whole lot in that file on the TVA, Senator."

Parting reluctantly from Mr. Barker, who though a Republican had voted for McKellar, the Senator eventually introduced a newspaperman who had talked to Chairman Dies about the letter, and didn't think it unused because illegally seized—"Half the stuff we used was got illegally," he quoted Dies. However, this witness had seen only a mimeographed copy.

When Mr. Hart at last arrived to talk about the letter attributed to him, he proved to be a surprisingly coherent and convincing witness. What made his case interesting was that, after his confession of party membership at the age of nineteen, and withdrawal at twenty-one, he had been allowed to keep his TVA job—four more years having passed before his error was disclosed. This had given McKellar opportunity throughout the hearings to say that TVA kept on its pay roll a confessed ex-Communist while firing a hundred-per-cent American just because he didn't like unions.

But Mr. Hart, though born in India, was no less American—his father had been a Y secretary stationed abroad during the first World War. His mother was head of the public speaking department at Vanderbilt. He had gone to Vanderbilt before working for TVA, but was now a graduate student at the University of Wisconsin. He had been an Army officer; and, since he was accepted for a commission, had assumed that his explanation of withdrawal from the Communist party had been accepted.

He had joined the party because he thought it stood for things he believed in at the time. He was intensely religious at that age; had spent the summer as an unpaid worker with the Quakers. At the time he joined the party, he was a member in good standing of the Methodist Church in Knoxville, and had specifically excepted religion from his temporary agreement with party tenets.

He was still in the Reserve and also an officer in the American Veterans Committee, where he had taken a stand against Communism. He freely acknowledged the youthful mistake he had made, back in 1936, when he was running an adding machine for TVA. He hadn't even seen Mr. Lilienthal then and knew Mr. Lilienthal had no idea who he was among all the employees.

No, he had never seen another person from TVA at the three party meetings he had attended. No, he wouldn't say the Spanish relief organization, in which he was especially interested, was Communist dominated—not in Knoxville. "There were some awfully respectable and decent and anti-Communist people in Knoxville who were helping the Spanish Loyalists."

[ 191 ]

As for the letter, it was a fabrication out of whole cloth and he had so described it in an affidavit made in 1943, before going into the Army. More, having given the matter some thought, he was able to point out obvious errors in the letter. It was signed Henry C. Hart, Jr., which he never signed because it wasn't his name—he had a different middle name from his father. It was dated on the day Mr. Smith, the man who lost his job, knew he had lost it; at that time he, Hart, had already left the party. The letter referred to the "Knoxville lodge of UFW," a designation used by AFL, not CIO members—he would have written Local 24 of UFW. Mr. Hart did not say so, but the phrase "their lodge" was used in Mr. Smith's testimony at the hearings.

If there had been any lingering doubt about the nature of the letter so many times brought into the record, the Hart testimony must have settled it. Mr. Hart did not even allow the Senator the satisfaction of proving through him that the Communist party was infiltrating CIO. "They would have been tickled to death to do it if they could," the witness admitted. But the union "would have been horror-struck if they had known that there was a Communist in the outfit."

There was, of course, further testimony intended to show that there were more than three Communists in TVA, although Chairman Hickenlooper remarked at one point that witnesses were not justifying the public expense. There was a nurse from Knoxville who, when her son failed to get a job with TVA, joined the Communist party to see if it were true that joining would help him.

It didn't, but she reported to Mr. Dies the names of TVA and Workers' Alliance people, and once she went to a meeting at the Farragut Hotel with these Communists—"and I guess maybe I shouldn't say Communists, I should say TVA employees," because the Communist meetings were "held in nigger shacks."

There was also the deputy sheriff from Knoxville, sworn in to look for violations—"any kind of violations." He told of shadowing one TVA employee—"I don't know whether it was TVA or some other section of the government, but he associated with fellows working for TVA. He went in and out of nights," and was allegedly a Communist, although, the witness confessed, "I have been informed that he married a niece of mine." Then, the witness continued, he had once gone out to Reeves' Roost to see some people, nudists they were, in bathing. "They were Communists but they didn't work for TVA." And there had been a man whose wife worked over at the old post office, who made loud speeches at the CIO meetings—but that wouldn't exactly be a Communist meeting, that was the CIO. "They got a whole lot of buildings that the government has got leased there, and they always give a fellow a job, I reckon, if he wants it. I don't know." One thing the witness did know: "We are proud of the TVA. It's brought millions there to our country and we are proud of it."

Diligent inquiry of many witnesses established that one TVA employee, besides the three Communist party members, had joined the Socialist party at fifteen and left it at seventeen. Another, the only employee in any important

[ 193 ]

post to be mentioned in the Dies hearings, had been definitely cleared, to become a major in Army Intelligence and win the Purple Heart. A third had become an adviser to Owen D. Young. "That well-known Communist?" asked Senator McMahon.

If the mention of all these witnesses who failed to establish Senator McKellar's point seems hardly relevant, it can be explained by the testimony of Mrs. Margaret Worrell, who, near the end of the hearings, explained that she spoke for the Women's Patriotic Conference on National Defense, a group of twenty-nine societies. "We are here," said Mrs. Worrell, "to oppose the appointment of David Eli Lilienthal to the Atomic Energy Commission, and of any other man against whom the finger of suspicion has been or can be pointed."

Senator Knowland asked the witness two questions: "Do you believe in the general Anglo-American theory that a person is innocent until proven guilty?" and "Do you not think it rather a dangerous doctrine that the Senate should withhold confirmation merely because the finger of suspicion, as you call it, is pointed at someone?"

Mrs. Worrell was unimpressed by these considerations, and she wanted to ask the Committee something else: "Has the Monsanto Chemical Company Atomic Plant under the Manhattan District been investigated *in re* communistic infiltration?" But the point raised by the Senator, after Lilienthal had spoken as an Anglo-American lawyer, is one that needed the public attention these hearings gave it. For ten years, ever since the first Dies hearings, the technique of accusation—say anything, no matter how un-

[ 194 ]

true, then demand that public servants be "like Caesar's wife"—had been used to deprive the American government of useful administrators. The appointment of David Lilienthal was the first one in which the farfetched accusations were faced, fought out, and publicly discredited. It was important, therefore, that the Senate committee should have listened to Mrs. Worrell and the Patriotic Conference, even though it was to be guided by the recommendation of the Association of University Women, the National Women's Trade Union League, the American Veterans Committee, the American Association for the United Nations, the Federal Council of Churches, the Presbyterians, the Unitarians, the Friends Committee, the Congregational Churches, the National Council of Jewish Women, and the many other organizations petitioning for confirmation.

Perhaps the senators were also mindful of the Gallup poll which showed citizens in general definitely for Lilienthal, with a few more Democrats than Republicans voting for him but with no significant difference between education groups.

This evidence of public sentiment was important because it showed that people all over the country, including the South, were not taken in by the Communism charge. Walter Lippmann asked in his column if the fact that a man was accused made him not above suspicion. Dorothy Thompson said David Lilienthal, "American Public Servant Number One," was "as much a Communist as the late Senator Norris." More important, Southern papers resented it, and began poking fun at the red scare. When

McKellar called Lilienthal "the chief Communist of my state" they were mad at the Senator but tickled too, because they knew both men. So the Birmingham *Age-Herald* said "The witch-hunt is backfiring," and Southern paragraphers wrote jokes about girls so scared of being called Communists that they put on bathing suits in the bathtub. When even the South refuses to get excited over charges like that, you can believe the fever is breaking.

During the hearings Lilienthal not only remained calm under foolish accusations, he took occasion to set the record straight about those that involved innocent people and organizations. Because the Southern Conference for Human Welfare opposes the poll tax, many Southern Democrats are against it; because Mrs. Roosevelt was among its sponsors, Republicans like to join in condemnation. But asked by Senator McKellar if he didn't know the conference was a Communist-front organization at the time one TVA director, former Senator Pope, attended a meeting at Chattanooga, Lilienthal said, "I did not know it then and I do not know it now." He explained that the organization had been started by the president of North Carolina University, by Chattanooga businessmen, and "a good many people of miscellaneous views and background, who felt that activity in the promotion of human welfare in the South was a worth-while undertaking." At one time, he recalled, Senator Bankhead of Alabama had spoken at a conference meeting—and "One gets a feeling of confidence about an organization which the late Senator Bankhead would address in Birmingham."

As far as real evidence went, the hearings were a waste

[ 196 ]

of time. The recommendations of all the important people could have come in by mail; after his first testimony seemed to produce no immediate effect, Dr. Karl Compton wrote in to repeat that he knew no one so well qualified as David Lilienthal, and to add:

However, my concern with the situation goes deeper than the fate of Lilienthal himself. He has won the respect and backing of the key people in the atomic energy development. Among them there is, so far as I can judge, a universal feeling of disillusionment and disgust over the manner in which the case has been handled by the Senate. . . .

Already the projects at Oak Ridge and Los Alamos have been severely reduced in effectiveness by the withdrawal of a large portion of the scientific personnel after the war. The shortage of competent scientists and the competition for their services are very great indeed, and practically all of the key men have many other offers, and most of them still on the job have stayed there from a sense of duty.

If however they become disillusioned, or gain the impression that political or special interests are getting control of the program, I believe that it will collapse into a rather hollow shell.

A letter from the scientists at Los Alamos confirmed this warning. But important as were the recommendations from the scientists and the industrialists, the most interesting people to come before the committee were a group of people up from the Valley in the last week of the hearings—people whose names you wouldn't know unless you knew that country.

There was a businessman from Knoxville, wanting to say a word for his neighbor, Mr. Lilienthal—he'd never been in Mr. Lilienthal's house, but he was proud to say that Mr. Lilienthal had been in his. There was a Chattanooga businessman, Joseph H. Lane, a corporation president. He believed atomic power was "the most serious thing in my life and my children's life," and he would trust David Lilienthal with it because he thought he was an honest man, "both mentally and morally," and a capable administrator. TVA, Mr. Lane said, had done a lot for private industry in the Valley. One of his factories was on the river bank; not only had the flood crest been reduced, high-water warnings had been accurate and helpful. TVA reforestation, bringing back the timber, would be good for his woodworking plant. Mr. Lane didn't take up the time of the senators to say so, but, underlining his present approval of TVA, he likes to tell how he once opposed it enough to bring his whole family down from Lookout Mountain in the rain to vote against TVA power in the Chattanooga bond election.

More witnesses included a newspaper publisher from Decatur, Alabama, and a banker from Florence, and an insurance man from Guntersville. The insurance man said that although to begin with people were rather skeptical, "I would say that practically all of the people believe TVA is a good thing," and "We feel that Mr. Lilienthal is an honest man and a true American." The banker remembered standing by the Shoals and saying, "What in the world will they ever do with all that power?" Mr. Lilienthal had said it would be insufficient, and in time it was, proving him a man of vision. The newspaper publisher recalled the time when seven out of eight banks failed, and he'd seen the changes since then. When a senator suggested that this improvement at the Shoals had come as a result of help from the taxpayers of the whole United States, he said he'd seen "considerable change in the thinking of the people." People had become "a great deal more confident about what we can do for ourselves."

There was the President of the Huntsville, Alabama, Chamber of Commerce—but to know the importance of what he said, you would have to remember how Huntsville felt about TVA, and David Lilienthal, ten years ago. There was a former TVA engineer, one of those big, solid engineers, who said proudly of the project he had worked on that "its accomplishments transcend anything of like nature which the world has ever previously seen," and, having been with the whole thing from the start, thought he knew how much of its success was due to Lilienthal's management. There was the man from the little town of Sweetwater, Tennessee, who had "never personally contacted any Communists in our section of the country"; he was there only to say that "I am not a prepared speaker and come from a rather small town, but my experience with Mr. Lilienthal and my belief and faith in him is that he is the man of the hour."

Or there was the man who never got to Washington at all, since he lived three miles up the side of a mountain on the other side of Oak Ridge. He had been a farmer at Wheat community, but when he had to move out he got a job as storekeeper for a mountain coal mine. He had read about the hearings in the papers and he was greatly relieved when Mr. Lilienthal was confirmed. Relieved, that is, for the country.

"I don't see why they had to say those things they said, though," objected his wife. "My great-grandfather was German, but I don't feel ashamed. Why—"

"Mr. Lilienthal came out all right," her husband said. "He can take care of himself."

# XI

*People are interested in personalities, and while it is true that seven-eighths of this has not been about what these men are going to administer if and when they are confirmed, nevertheless there have probably been a good many people who have begun to absorb some of the problems that are implied in the atomic energy field.*

> SENATOR BRIAN MCMAHON at hearings of the Atomic Energy Committee on confirmation of the Commission.

IN DAVID LILIENTHAL'S STUDY there is a little duck. It is a calm and pleasant but very confident duck; in a nice, ducky way it is cocking a snoot. Made out of modeling clay, it has been shellacked so that it affords a perfect illustration of the water-off-a-duck's-back analogy. It is appropriate that this should be Lilienthal's contribution to the art of sculpture, for if ever a man needed its qualities he is that man. To some extent, at least, he has them.

Starting with the acute sensitivity that comes naturally to perceptive people, in the early days he blushed visibly, not in shame but in wrath, at some of the more preposterous charges made in political trials. Now, relaxed, he has learned not only to weather criticism but to welcome it as only part of the job. "Don't put me down as a martyr," he told an AP reporter during the Congressional hearings.

Not Lilienthal but Congress was on trial in the long squabble—Congress and the ability of the American people to tell their Washington representatives what to do. Considered from that standpoint, the hearings and the debates in both houses took on an importance far beyond any person's job, though not, of course, beyond the importance of atomic energy.

Looking on the dark side, one obvious disclosure was the inability of certain legislators to understand the importance of the subject; there was a simple technological time lag in the Congressional mind. Of this Senator McKellar's reiterated question "Should we give this bomb secret away, without money and without price?" was the perfect example. The Senator, first of all, couldn't understand the scientific warning that the "secret" wasn't patentable. Next, he couldn't realize that the whole question was beyond any consideration of dollars and cents. One of the witnesses he badgered told him this, but the Senator's attitude toward witnesses was that of the county prosecutor; he tartly rebuked Dr. Karl Compton for the errors of the Weather Bureau.

As an exhibition of individual senility the McKellar attitudes were no more than embarrassing to the human race, but as a disclosure of governmental dilapidation they were a threat to the country. Senatorial courtesy, it was explained, required that the septuagenarian from Tennessee be allowed to waste weeks of working people's time and to dominate the proceedings of a committee on which he had no seat. This was discouraging to those aware that democratic procedures, in a world which does not always wait for the worst tricks of parliamentarianism, are still on trial.

Specifically the McKellar case was one more example of the political frustration of the South and was so recognized by Southern papers. "How long, O Lord, how long?" asked the Greensboro, N. C., *News,* "How long will the South continue to be misrepresented by the Bilbos, Rankins, and McKellars?" In the course of the hearings the Senator himself read into the record a series of wrathful reproaches from the poll-tax states, of which the remark of the Chattanooga *Times*—"The sensible people of Tennessee hang their heads in shame at the spectacle Senator McKellar is making of himself"—was typical.

More important than Congressional procedure or the poll-tax problem was the fact disclosed in the hearings that Congress in general was, if not as ignorant as McKellar, still fumbling and uncertain in its approach to the new power. Here a good comment was made by the Washington *Post:*

The opposition to Mr. Lilienthal developing among ultra-conservative Republicans and Southern democrats is in reality an opposition to the atomic-energy law which Congress itself enacted last year. The awe inspired by discovery of the cosmic force inherent in nuclear fission has now somewhat diminished. And accordingly there has set in a reaction from the high-mindedness which prompted Congress to treat atomic energy as a stupendous gift of nature to be exploited only under public authority for the general welfare. In its place is an enterprise-as-usual attitude which would treat the atom as just another invention—a new type of plastic, say, or a synthetic fuel—and turn it over to private exploitation for profit. But the Senate, at least, was unanimous in its statesmanship last year. Those who now deplore the statesmanship dare not challenge the law. So they seek instead to set aside Mr. Lilienthal because he is an administrator who believes in the law and would enforce it.

This explanation of Congressional behavior holds water better than some of those which, comparing the delay in confirmation of Lilienthal's appointment with other disputed nominations, found several famous parallels. The fight over the Brandeis appointment to the Supreme Court was most often mentioned but had, perhaps, least relevance; beyond the fact that both men were good lawyers, and both Jewish, and both bore themselves well and spoke eloquently under unworthy attack, there was no close parallel. There was a tough fight, too, over the confirmation of Justice Hughes, whose handicap was only that he was a Republican.

More apposite was the defeat of Thomas R. Amlie for the Interstate Commerce Commission because, as a Progressive Republican from Wisconsin, he was called a socialist. To some minds it would seem that one believer in government ownership of railroads, on a fifteen-man board charged with railroad regulation, would not constitute a menace. But a Democratic Congress so voted.

The fight against Lilienthal as an alleged left-winger was absurd but, interpreted, it did mean that Congress thought he could not be controlled. The people working hardest against him were people believing earnestly not merely in free business enterprise but in the right of industry to tell the government what to do. Witness the fact that the first atomic-power bill, which would have left the problem in the hands of the generals and of their good friend in the ranks, Private Enterprise, was brought in by Congressman May of Kentucky. A later move in the course of the Congressional fight, proposing to abolish the Commission in favor of control by existing government departments, was introduced by another old enemy of TVA, Congressman Jenkins of Ohio. Southern papers which saw the whole thing as another attack on TVA, instigated by the power lobby or the fertilizer industry, were looking from a local angle but their generalization was sound: the core of opposition to Lilienthal was in the fact that responsible administration of atomic energy control would curb private exploitation of the new processes.

That Congress would be moved by such considerations is inconceivable if it is assumed that a direct relationship must be established between any great corporation wishing to use an Oak Ridge process, and, say, Senator Taft, who led the opposition to Lilienthal on the Senate floor. No such relationship is implied. What is evident is that senators like Mr. Taft are moved by the political principles of a prebomb, precartel era, when the worst a great corporation could do was charge too much for light or freight. Mr. Taft's dismissal as "Communist propaganda" of what he called "the widespread notion that there is no defense against the atomic bomb" was not only an insult to scientific opinion, it was an insult to the common sense of any

[ 205 ]

person living in a world of airplanes. Nobody should feel insulted, because the Senator did not mean it so, but everybody should worry when a man in Mr. Taft's important position shows so little awareness of the world.

Whether or not Senator Vandenberg knows more of world problems, he is a closer observer of public-opinion polls and he had the galleries with him when he made his speech in public disagreement with Mr. Taft. Mr. Barkley of Kentucky also put the matter well when he said that in his day he had been accused of socialistic leanings. And it was worth noting that the voting cut right across party lines, with Republicans for and of course some Democrats against.

In the House, where they had no vote but did plenty of talking, there were freak divisions, too. You had Representative Crawford of Michigan, who would like not only to keep the bombs in Army hands but to use them, voting the way he naturally would. You had Mr. Busby bringing the whole Lilienthal family into it the way they used to do with the Roosevelts, except that by some oversight he missed the fact that Mr. Lilienthal's little dog, Penny, is a cocker spaniel with copper-red hair. On the other hand you had Representative Rankin of Mississippi keeping quiet because he knows the value of TVA.

The whole thing should be instructive to politicians in somewhat the same way the case of Congressman John Jennings of Tennessee has been. Mr. Jennings started out as a lawyer on the power-company side in the fight against TVA, but when he went into politics he changed over and promised, as a condition of election, to fight just as hard for the Authority as he had fought against it. Other Valley politicians, always excepting Senator McKellar, have found that there is no use going against the people on an issue known to affect public welfare. If that is true of TVA it is even more true of atomic energy; the only question is whether the country has time to educate the politicians who constitute the biggest problem in the atomic energy field.

We have to give Congress credit for passing one good act, the McMahon bill, despite knowledge that it was what Senator Hickenlooper called the greatest "centralization of governmental and bureaucratic power that this country has ever passed in peacetime." It could, the Senator admitted, mean that we were in some way building a change in our economy. This above all things is what senators dread, but the smarter ones realized there had been a big change in applied physics. They were brought to this realization by the scientists themselves, who came out of the laboratories long enough to talk in a way understandable to plain people. More, they were quoted in the newspapers.

This was a matter on which Lilienthal had made himself clear before he was nominated. In an article published in *The Progressive Farmer,* back in 1945, he said the real question was "whether the people will be permitted to know enough about Atomic Energy so that they can participate in the decisions about it":

There may be those who will feel that the social and economic consequences of the development of peacetime use of Atomic Energy will be so disastrous to some investors that the

[ 207 ]

development of Atomic Energy should not be pressed beyond the military phase. In other words, we don't dare tell the people what the possibilities are because of its effect upon the stock market, upon this-or-that business, perhaps upon social institutions. These are the "Papa knows best" people. They will feel that the facts should be fed out to the people only as those of superior wisdom feel is best. Their motives they will describe to themselves as being of the highest. They don't want the people to be hurt!

Now, whether such people are called social planners or big business tycoons, they represent a lack of faith in people—a lack of faith in the responsibility of science and scientific development to count the people in. Therefore, I think that high on the list of public discussion should be the question:

*Are the people going to be told what the best scientific and technical brains know about the potentialities and therefore the social and economic consequences of future developments? Or are these facts going to be kept in the hands of the "Papa knows best" group, whoever they may be?*

Another question is of a similar character. It may be that the people will be told that the development of this energy, while a great success for war where the cost is unimportant, is economically unfeasible. Will there be a public declaration at the proper time as to the basis for that conclusion? Will we be told that by economically unfeasible is meant that it will be too disruptive of existing investment both large and small, investment in huge factory equipment or in the farmer's small tractor? Will we be told what adjustments would have to be made, what existing investment would have to be scrapped or become obsolete? Will the people have a chance to decide by the process of public discussion whether that cost is too great and therefore that Atomic Energy is uneconomic and therefore unfeasible? Or will the public be given a great run-around on this subject? Will the people have a chance to think about it with all the consequences before them and do their own reckoning on social consequences?

In the Congressional controversy the papers printed the news and four-fifths of them took a stand for Lilienthal. More, they took occasion to comment on the attitude of Congress not only toward the nominees, but toward public safety in world affairs. The Nashville *Tennessean* said "A serious question as to the extent to which the Senate has been converted to the cause of collective security has been raised by the Lilienthal hearings," and the Philadelphia *Bulletin* remarked, "If all persons who can be called friendly to the Russians are barred from office, our relations with the Soviets are certain to deteriorate."

It was one case where you couldn't tell whether the papers were influencing the people or the other way around, because public opinion and the editorial writers moved together. When you have outspoken support from all the experts and the churches and both wings of labor and the *Daily News,* and opposition from the people whose letters are unsigned and unprintable, you are doing all right. The real danger is that people could come to rely too much on Lilienthal as a safe administrator, and not think enough about the problems that remain to be solved.

Take the veto question, which came up in the hearings when Senator Knowland said, "I cannot conceive that the Senate would ever approve a situation in which the veto was there." This no doubt is a sound estimate of senatorial sentiment, but before the Russians began arguing for a veto, you could say as certainly—some people did say—that the Senate would never approve international control of anything without reserving its right to say no. The reservations by which the Senate wanted to nullify the old League of Nations were a fancy way of claiming the veto power which the Russians claim today, and it is hard to escape a suspicion that they have been jockeyed into saying what the Senate must otherwise have said. Or has the Senate, moved by anti-Soviet feeling, been forced into a contrary but unnatural attitude?

Or take the question that Lilienthal himself raised in the farm paper—for whom is the public development of atomic energy "unfeasible"? All through the hearings commentators toyed with that problem, naming only "power interests" in general, though Mrs. Roosevelt said right out "one begins to wonder who pulls the strings." But you could perhaps figure it for yourself from different angles. Power nowadays is not just coal or rivers, it is literally what the copybooks said it was, knowledge. That knowledge was and still is in the minds of men loaned to the government, in many cases, by big corporations who were already interested in the sort of research into heavy chemicals and light metals that the war speeded up. It seems safe to assume that what these big corporations wanted before the war they would still like to have. According to the American way of life as many congressmen still see it, they are entitled to that ownership even if it involves atomic power patents.

Considering this, the public should make up its mind

whether it wants the corporations to have what they want, or whether the exploding atom is a good place to draw the line. In making this decision the public should consider not only the various charges of communism or socialist opinion made against individuals in Congressional hearings, but the proofs of industrial collaboration with I. G. Farbenindustrie unearthed during the war by what was then the Truman committee.

It is important to keep these things in mind because the opposition to Lilienthal will not stop with failure to block his nomination. Already the threat has gone out that the Commission will be strangled in the time-honored Congressional manner, by cutting off funds. There would be support for this not only from the legislators who want the corporations to have what they want, and from those who want the Army to have what it wants, but from the innocent small minds that think you should save the taxpayer money in the atomic energy field.

The opposition to Lilienthal is no new thing: it has been going on since the Wisconsin days when "Get Lilienthal" was the slogan in a state fight; and it continued all through the TVA days, even as late as 1945. It was in that year, according to a story told by Senator Taylor of Idaho, that he made a trip to the Valley and heard a long conversation among carousing congressmen who were, at the moment, enjoying the hospitality of a big corporation. Between drinks poured by the company representative they were still saying "Get Lilienthal."

Fortunately there are people on the other side, sober and responsible people, to say we are lucky to get Lilienthal to take the hardest job assignment of all time. Professional observers by no means unfavorable to corporate interests have recognized, in this instance, that an administrator of Lilienthal's experience was required. It was Walter Lippmann who said, "It is the administration of an enormously valuable material resource and public property in collaboration with private corporations and private individuals, involving scientific research and both civil and military service. Mr. Lilienthal happens to be the only man in the United States who has ever administered such a big and special project."

Going beyond the ordinary administrative requirements, an editorial writer down in Montgomery, Alabama, said, of all the men named to the Atomic Energy Commission, "Nor should their vision and loyalty be confined solely to national boundaries. Their vision must transcend the present, and their loyalty must be large enough, and deep enough, to embrace all of mankind. Else this thing atomic energy will be our death, and the world's."

Speaking for himself, Lilienthal said only that he had some experience in administering a public project on which "the problem of harmonizing and getting things accomplished through technicians was an important part of the job." He added, "I am not an expert on atomic energy now and I would think that I could hardly expect to be in the future, in a scientific sense." But he had been a painstaking administrator of public business, although he did not say this, ever since he told the Lions and Kiwanis at Sheboygan, Michigan, in 1933, that "when we are thinking of how to improve the regulatory mechanism which we

[ 212 ]

have worked out tentatively for the control of one kind of business, the public utilities, we should bear in mind that we are doing more than merely learning to regulate public utilities. By a method of trial and error which is a characteristically American method, we are devising a technique of community control of every business which directly and immediately affects the public welfare."

It is just as well to have at the head of the Atomic Energy Commission a man who has already gone through the trials and errors and devised his technique. And it seems reasonable to hope that as the methods first tried out in Wisconsin worked for a larger area, in the Valley, so the TVA techniques will if properly adapted work for the world. For States' rights read national rights; for federal government read United Nations; for power companies read cartels. For the people of the Valley, struggling against handicaps, suspicious of new techniques and frightened by tremendous changes, read the people of the world. In either case, the problems of human administration—Lilienthal's problems—loom larger than the scientific problems, which specialists are equipped to solve faster than men can make use of the solutions.

As TVA was a pioneer development, atomic energy is pioneering on a larger, more strenuous scale. You can look at David Lilienthal and say here is a man who will always be a pioneer, ready to move on to something better ahead, instead of establishing himself in one selected spot and confining his subsequent activities to Old Settlers' Week. Except, of course, that it's hard to see where he will go after the atom adventure.

As a pioneer he has a quality which some of the early American settlers, by reputation, lacked—flexibility. "A corporation clothed with the power of government but possessed of the flexibility and initiative of a private enterprise," said President Roosevelt in his famous message establishing the Tennessee Valley Authority. In the early days of TVA, the flexibility which it needed was supplied by David Lilienthal. And for modern administration as for modern building, flexibility is a quality to be relied on, not distrusted. It is considered a virtue, not a defect, in the newest of the big dams that its top shifts a measurable fraction of an inch when the sun strikes its face.

To say that Lilienthal had in Wisconsin and in the early days in Tennessee some of the qualities he will need from now on is not of course to say that he has not improved these qualities. Visitors to his first TVA office were always attracted to an eight-foot desk built like a drawing table, before which Lilienthal's chair, on easy rolling casters, moved up and down. It was his design, but he didn't stop with one model. Now in the Washington office there is another desk, made of the laminated lumber that is a successful Valley experiment, with its ends rounded to enclose the chair. "In thirteen years," says Lilienthal, "I learned to sit still and curve the desk."

The day he said that, the Washington office was keyed to high excitement because the Senate was voting, too close, to confirm Gordon Clapp as Lilienthal's successor in the Valley. One useful trait in an administrator is to be able to pick good people and have them stay on their jobs, working not only for him but with each other. The book

*TVA: Democracy on the March* reveals the writer's consciousness of what business calls the personnel problem, as well as his success in solving it. He said to a university audience, when he first came to the Valley, that a new democracy must "utilize the services of technically trained men." He had experts in the Wisconsin power commission, they had more experts at TVA. As chairman Lilienthal learned, he admits, that specialists working against each other can create problems of their own. But fortunately specialists are people, and Lilienthal has always been able to get on with them, as with the farmers, by an understanding of their problems combined with an unpretentiousness to which all TVA men will testify. In the early dam-buildings days, they noticed that when Lilienthal came to look over a job he didn't just drive up like a boss and leave his car anywhere, he asked, like any ordinary considerate person, where to park. Not long ago Charles Krutch, TVA's artist-photographer, put it down as a relevant fact that in all the years at Knoxville he had never seen Lilienthal's Phi Beta Kappa key.

In the atomic energy business the new chairman of the new Commission will need tact, because he has inherited the most important group of technicians in the world, and their nerves are already frayed. Some of them didn't like making bombs to begin with. They distrusted, as time went on, the political proprietorship that took over their work. As soon as they could, many of the best men left the government. One of the important Oak Ridge scientists who is still there, Dr. Paul Henshaw, has worked hard outside his laboratory, talking to students and helping to educate public opinion; but last spring he complained to a New York *Times* reporter that the country had wasted eighteen months of its two-to-five year lead over the rest of the world. "And we seem to be getting nowhere at all in the most important field of all, the development of political controls. How much more time can we afford to waste?"

Lilienthal has said that the Commission is trying to hire back some of the men who went away, and of course it may succeed. But in this respect the problem is the reverse of the one TVA had in '33, when every good engineer in the country was looking for a job.

Another problem in dealing with the scientists is, as Lilienthal has already pointed out, that the Commission must ask them to work in the dark, publishing no papers and teaching no classes what they know. As control gets under way this condition should attract to an Atomic Energy Authority, as the State Department report suggests, those who wish to work at the center of knowledge. But meanwhile Lilienthal has expressed his own realization that under the restrictions the atomic program could "become a fine nesting place for industrious mediocrity." On the hopeful side, it was the top scientists in the country who fought to have Lilienthal appointed and confirmed; they should stand by to the extent of working when called upon to do so by the Commission they endorsed.

Still another consideration for "Operation Headache" is financial; already, it is said, much of the first two billion invested in the Manhattan Project must be written off because, as atomic science advances, equipment grows obsolete. Lilienthal can explain that to senators to whom, in the Valley, he could show dams built to last forever.

TVA did have a problem at Muscle Shoals, and the Muscle Shoals plant—built for war, and not too useful as it stood even for that—was the best parallel for the atomic energy situation as it is at present. This is encouraging, because you will find farmers in the Valley now who set more store by the phosphate fertilizers than by the cheap electricity. "It's the phosphates that did it," they'll tell you, looking at the green fields.

David Lilienthal learned about these useful down-to-earth ways of helping farmers in his years in the South. Wisconsin taught him how to run a technical job, picking good people and standing up under the fire of criticism. The first years in the Valley perhaps taught him some things not to do, however well meant. But the later years were at once years of bigger opportunities, of relationships with the whole world as it came to the TVA door, and of a new neighborly knowledge of the Tennessee earth that is, of course, like the land in other parts. Lilienthal liked to watch Wisconsin farmers and Alabama farmers get together and talk about phosphates; he liked to brag a little himself, as he admitted out in Oregon, about the Tennessee Valley. But he may not realize himself, in spite of the agriculture award, what a good Southern farmer he got to be. The proof is a Lilienthal plan to retire, someday, to a farm in Tennessee or north Georgia and raise cattle—a plan, of course, that implies such success on the present job as will make it safe to count on living anywhere.

If the Atomic Energy Commission can eventually turn

[ 217 ]

Oak Ridge and Los Alamos and Hanford to work as useful as the phosphates were, if they can spread out the beneficial effects of atomic energy in the same way, so that different nations will benefit as did the different states, and if eventually the countries of the world can learn the sort of co-operation that the Valley farmers learned—then, of course, the problem is solved. The world will be as peaceful as Pickwick Landing on the Tennessee, where they once fought the battle of Shiloh.

Recalling the record of the Biblical David, you can say as people have said that in taming the river Lilienthal slew one giant—he himself called the unbridled Tennessee "an idle giant and a destructive one." There, as the earlier David could face the giant because he had already met a lion and a bear, he had to meet first the lionlike opposition of Dr. Arthur Morgan, who attacked with a reverberating roar, and the bearlike tactics of Wendell Willkie, who sought first to smother the infant Tennessee Valley Authority and then to sweep it out of his way with one push of his paw.

But you get a better understanding of present problems if you impersonalize the issues and say that the lion in the path was older ideas of right and property and propriety, still strong and kingly in appearance, as noble in decay as the lion on the shield of a declining empire. You have to respect the lion but you must not yield to him. As for the bear, a likable big beast, whimsical in his ways, unpredictable in temper and so dangerous too, but worst when roused from a long winter sleep—who is that beast but public inertia, only too given to hibernation, but always

[ 218 ]

threatening emergence and impulsive action; still unde-
cided whether to lead a private or a public life?

The giant today, of course, is what they are fond of
calling the giant atom. Like the dams, it can be neither
good nor evil in itself—only big. But there it is beside the
river, with a lot of people afraid to touch it, wishing they
could forget it.

There it is, growing no smaller. There are fewer people
employed at Oak Ridge than at the peak of wartime production, that is true. But the consumption of TVA power
has passed the war output, and it isn't all going into making
nylons, in the Valley.

## XII

*Be careful, my dear brother, don't take away the joy,*
*But use it for the good of man, and never to destroy.*

*Atomic power, atomic power,*
*It was given by the mighty hand of God.* . . .

Song, "Atomic Power," by FRED KIRBY

WHEN you have looked hard at David Lilienthal's record
for twenty-five years back, you get a sense of confidence
about him in his new job, but it is just as well not to relax
and be too happy. It isn't the same job he had as chairman
of TVA, in spite of the parallels.

Perhaps it is too easy for readers of the State Department
report to confuse the international Atomic Energy Authority there proposed with the actual Atomic Energy Commission of the United States. The international authority,
as Lilienthal told the United Nations control committee,
would when created have as its prime purpose "the elim-
ination of national rivalries in the dangerous aspects of
the development of atomic energy." In contrast, the purpose of the present United States commission is "to develop atomic energy along lines of research, engineering
improvements and the production of fissionable materials
and weapons on behalf of the United States of America,"

although "the people of the United States have indicated in the strongest terms" their preference for an international system.

There is encouragement in the action which, less than a year after establishment of the United States commission and only a little more than two years after Hiroshima, offered the world the first obvious gain from atomic energy: radioactive isotopes for use in research. This move, welcomed not only by foreign scientists but by informed opinion in the United States, was in keeping with Lilienthal policies and might have been forecast by anyone familiar with the policies of the whole Commission.

Other international news of the same date emphasized the value of the isotope offer. A British cabinet minister was appealing, without chance of success, for a division of gold reserves; yet in terms of actual usefulness to humanity, isotopes for fighting disease can be more valuable than all the gold in Fort Knox. With political motives openly announced, the United States was making or withholding gifts of munitions and supplies, not always to the complete satisfaction even of the favored nations. The offer of the isotopes was peaceful and non-political, and without discrimination as long as announced conditions were accepted. One of these conditions, that countries using the isotopes "permit qualified scientists irrespective of nationality to visit the institutions where the materials will be used," neatly by-passed the problem of international inspection upon which the United Nations Atomic Energy Commission still disagreed.

Objectors to the Commission's action—the New York

*Daily Mirror* headlined "Peril for U.S. in 'Atom Gifts' "—
were people who could be counted upon to oppose all
international cooperation; they reacted in the same way to
Roosevelt's gift of old destroyers in World War II. "Experts" referred to in the scareheads turned out to be the
group for which Senator McKellar had been spokesman.
Scientists were quick to point out various factors which
made the offer safe, and conservative political observers
could see the advantage in any move to lessen distrust of
America's atomic monopoly which could be made without
threat to security. Although all action in the atomic field
takes courage, the sharing of information and research material has long been considered a scientific obligation and
is routine procedure in other fields. Newspaper accounts of
the isotope offer were paralleled by columns reporting
American results with a Russian method in cancer research, given international try-out as a matter of course.

But even if the isotopes do as much for the morale of
peace as Roosevelt's destroyers did for the morale of war,
problems remain to make Lilienthal's job a tough one.
In Knoxville the TVA offices were light and airy, with
plain painted walls. In Washington the offices of the
Atomic Energy Commission are impressive, but they are
paneled with dark knotted pine and the knots, so far,
seem to belong there. Lilienthal takes what consolation he
can from the fact that the building used to be, and still is
called, the Public Health Building. But they've got it full
of uniformed guards now, with visitors registered and
badged just as if they kept a stock of U-235 there that
could be taken out in a brief case.

The country's bomb plants and the stock piles are in the

hands of a civilian commission, and that was a great victory. Among the available civilians Lilienthal was not only the man most experienced, he was and is unmistakably a civilian clear through—human, unstarched, at times outspoken. You can sympathize as he struggles with the machinery of his job—hearings and appropriation fights and uncertainty of tenure as reappointment time comes around. You can realize that his problem isn't just managing the atom, it's persuading congressmen that scientists asked to do a tough job, and give up fat private-industry salaries to do it, may expect to be paid even more than a congressman, and may be worth more, to the country.

You can feel happy about what Lilienthal would like to do with the whole atomic energy business. Every page of the State Department report and all his speeches show that the hope of the Commission is to turn the whole thing to peaceful productive use. The reports aren't too specific, but it appears that what they have, or hope to have, is a brand new kind of power—not for trolleys or helicopters, but for power stations—that could do for the hard-up and backward countries of the world what river power is doing for the Tennessee Valley. You see how the theory applies: back in the early 30's Lilienthal was explaining in the Valley how prosperity, in the modern world, was measured almost directly in terms of power and the "value added" to raw materials by manufacture.

Some people seem to think that a world in which power was available for freer use would be a world of gadgets and industrial plants, but the Tennessee Valley is there to show you it isn't so. It can be a world of good farm land instead,

[ 223 ]

with the farmers wearing shoes. More, the wide waste lands of the world, the washed-out farm lands and the deserts, could in time be added to the green and fertile lands where people can live.

That should be considered by those whose minds shy off from the whole atomic idea because they don't like to think of Hiroshima and Nagasaki. That reluctance is understandable, although you can see the point made by one Oak Ridge scientist who suggests that what we did to the Japanese cities may help to convince the world that no war, even a war we wage ourselves, is good or civilized, or amenable to gentlemen's rules.

And though nobody wants to think of Hiroshima, unless it's the people in Washington who had a party with an angel food cake in the shape of an atomic explosion, you could afford to forget Hiroshima and the cake eaters too if you could see clearly that a big peacetime application of power was ready to help the overworked ordinary people of the world. Shinto legend told the Japanese that civilization came from the sun. Like all religious legend, that was a wish that could come true, letting the world start new with the flash of cosmic power in the sky.

Or, looking clear away from where we used the bomb, the Chinese when you think of it have a better case against American armed power than the Japanese have. China might have been glad to settle for two cities destroyed, in place of years of bombardment by New York elevated scrap iron powered by Texas oil. China needs power, more, even, than she can get by harnessing her rivers, TVA style. The same is true of India. Tamed and tractable atomic power would be our best ambassador of good will in that part of the world.

Or look if you like at the English, using what power they have to make goods for export, but looking ahead with shudders to another long cold winter, with the country not yet rebuilt. One atom-power station, if it were practical, could do more than they've ever been able to do with coal mines to warm the electric grid.

You don't have to be a wide-eyed idealist to feel that giving the nations who need it most a chance to use a universally applicable power would do away with the stresses that cause war. They say that Germany's Von Ribbentrop, learning in the Nuremberg jail what had happened at Hiroshima, was taken aback by the political application: Hitler, if only he had waited, couldn't have shouted about *Lebensraum*. The coal and steel barons who backed the Nazis wouldn't have had supreme power and the people who wanted American-style cars and British-style raincoats, like Der Fuehrer's, might have had them and stayed snug at home.

All these things, the scientists say, are in the future of atomic energy—if it has a future. But ask David Lilienthal about the *foreseeable* future and he won't underwrite any specific development. He has said, "There seems to me to be a definite value in avoiding speculation which may raise false and unobtainable hopes or cause pessimism about the future potentialities of atomic energy in the ordinary life of men."

But he knows that scientic inventions must change ways of living, calls for social inventions to match—hopes we may "develop a democratic way to meet these new and puzzling problems of the relationship of people to technical advances." In the TVA days he counted formation of the first farmers' co-op to distribute power as important as the first town contract to take power from TVA. In the State Department report there are specific recommendations for international distribution of atomic power. Having made these recommendations, Lilienthal is reluctant to make political prophecies, just as he can't say when this country will have an Arkansas Valley Authority even though TVA proved it would be a good idea.

As a democrat must, he hands the political problems back for the people to decide. In this case the people are not only Valley farmers and businessmen but the nations of the world; and that is why Lilienthal's speech to the Atomic Energy Commission of the United Nations sounded to some people as hard-boiled as the speech he made years ago at Chattanooga, warning that new power developments would depend on the people's use of power. What he actually said at Lake Success, if you looked beyond scare headlines, was:

Until there is international accord on this problem and international safeguards satisfactory to the nations of the world, the purpose of the United States Atomic Energy Commission is to maintain and indeed increase the pre-eminence of the United States of America in the field of the development of atomic energy and atomic weapons.

This is not saying that the Commission wants to make bombs; it is saying that the alternate to making bombs is international agreement.

At Chattanooga fourteen years before he had said, "As Americans we cling to the Jeffersonian principle of the right of the people to choose the kind of community and industrial life which to them seems good," and had quoted from Jane Addams about the two essentials of government, "truth and the consent of the people." In deciding what to do about atomic energy, you have to worry mainly over the difficulty of getting the people and the truth together, because many people feel they don't understand the problem and are too busy to learn more. One of the most frightening things since the bomb fell is a public-opinion survey made at the time of the Bikini tests and published by Cornell University. It was found that although 98 per cent of those questioned had heard of the bomb, nearly a third knew nothing of the United Nations. It was not, then, surprising that a majority voted to "keep the secret of the bomb." More than a third thought that the United States would be able to work out a defense against the bomb before other countries could learn how to make it, and of this overhopeful third the notion of possible defense was as prevalent among persons at high levels of general information as among the uninformed. Most discouraging of all was a general reluctance to think about the bomb, either through fatalism—"There is no use worrying about something you can't help"—or in false optimism: "I think the head officials or whatever it is would know how to use it." *

That is too much confidence to have even in David Lilienthal. Conversely, it is his confidence in people, in

* Quoted by Sylvia Eberhart in *Bulletin of the Atomic Scientists*, June, 1947.

their right to decide and their ability to decide right, that is Lilienthal's great strength—and, it could be, his big mistake. When you talk to him, and talk about him to other people, to those who have worked with him in offices or to the farmers in the Valley, to his friends and his secretaries and his family, you begin to say, "But what is wrong with the man? There must be *something* wrong. There must be somebody, besides Dr. Arthur Morgan and Senator McKellar, who doesn't like him. There must be something he does that he shouldn't, if it's only to swear at a senator or leave the cap off the toothpaste."

Then, if you look long enough, you begin to see one flaw, or what could be a flaw, for yourself. It's this: David Lilienthal really believes in people. He is a democrat with a little *d,* a possible fault, because, unless you share his faith in the wisdom of the people, you think there may come a time when the people or their representatives will tell him wrong.

Back in 1933 in the Tennessee Valley, warning that "we have seen one country after another abandon the democratic principle for some form of dictatorship," Lilienthal emphasized his fundamental assumption that "progress must come through the people, and not be imposed upon them." When the efficiency of TVA was cited as an example of successful "managerial revolution" Lilienthal, as chairman, was quick to answer back that it was nothing of the sort. All the way he has sought to avoid what Robert de St. Jean, writing after the fall of France, described as the tragedy of his generation—"little by little, in our country, we have seen the idea of democracy completely divorced

from the idea of efficiency." So far, his democratic determination has not stopped Lilienthal from effective administration; it remains to be seen whether popular intelligence can avert calamity on a world scale.

He himself recognizes that people need to have the right
information if they are to direct public affairs. That was
what led him to say, in his talk about atomic energy to the
Inland Daily Press Association at Chicago:

This can become a golden opportunity or a source of catas-
trophe, and the choice between the two depends, in my
opinion, chiefly upon the fundamental premise I have been
urging upon you—namely, that the public must become informed. So this is the first point in my answer to the wholly
intelligent and quite natural response of the average citizen
when he says "What can I do about it?" My answer is: "You
and I and all of us must first become informed. We must have
knowledge about this subject."

Although he said in the same speech that it was the
Atomic Energy Commission's job to pound away at the
problem of letting the people know, he added that

Responsibility for the presentation and interpretation of
the facts about atomic energy should *not* be vested in any
federal government agency, whether legislative or executive,
and it should not be the function of the Atomic Energy
Commission—except for the safeguarding of America's secret
technical knowledge. It is rather a task for the educational
institutions of the country, of which the press is the key
institution.

It was after this speech that a Chicago column asked plaintively "Dear Dave: We agree that the public ought to understand about atomic energy, but can you wait till we've mastered the mechanics of the zipper?" But Lilienthal argued that the facts necessary to grasp the essentials of the new processes were no more complicated than those required for ordinary public discussion "around every cracker barrel and every soda fountain and in every school and press room in this country. As a matter of fact, to keep the box score of a baseball game at Comiskey Park or to figure out batting averages seems to me a formidable undertaking compared to acquiring an understanding of the essential facts which the public needs about atomic energy."

This is true if you consider only the facts needed to show that you have to have control, or to know that you haven't got a "secret," or any defense that will protect people who happen to be underneath when an atomic bomb is dropped by an enemy plane. You can read the newspapers and find out the extent of Bikini damage, the fact that they haven't yet been able to "decontaminate" the ships, and judge for yourself whether you want to be attacked that way, even if the Army should find a way to win the war.

Or, you can use your common sense and, counting what we owe the foreign scientists who started cracking atoms, understand that further developments might occur to them, too. As he once said about a river and state lines, Lilienthal says now that a scientific fact "pays no attention to national boundaries. There are no such things as American neutrons, say, and some different kind of Russian neutrons, and British neutrons. A neutron doesn't know about boundary lines."

But suppose that despite the best efforts of the Commission and the 80 per cent efforts of the press, people are still misled by the loud-talking fabricators of delusion and fomenters of war? Suppose Congress votes wrong or directs wrong, in those joint sessions of its committee with the Commission. Suppose Congressional respect for the military reasserts itself, at a time of crisis in relations with other countries?

In the hearings, Chairman Hickenlooper asked whether Lilienthal ever evinced "a desire to shelve the reasonably necessary military applications in favor of devotion of the complete program to entirely civilian use?" And the witness, Charles A. Thomas, a vice-president of the Monsanto Chemical Company, said, "No, I don't think so at all. I think Mr. Lilienthal has a very firm understanding that to keep ahead in the military you must keep ahead in the industrial, in the practical applications." To prove his point Mr. Thomas went on to apply the lesson of the German dye firms in the first World War, who converted so quickly to poison gas and explosives.

More, under questioning Lilienthal himself said

I think it ought to be recognized at the outset, without any attempt to pull punches, that atomic energy at the present time and from the point of view of what seems to me to be the work of the Commission, is essentially a weapon of war; that it is the greatest weapon that has ever been devised and the most potent.

Later, asked about co-operation with the military, he said

It is quite impossible, as we see it, to say that at almost any stage, from raw materials to active material, there is not some military aspect to this problem, one that requires the interweaving of the military viewpoint.

It is not just a matter of having military advice at the point where one constructs a gadget in which to put the active material. From raw materials through separation processes, through plutonium, to the whole research and development and manufacturing operation, the views and the plans, the war plans, of the military are an inseparable part of this problem.

And our conception of the Division of Military Application is that of a major staff function in which the Director and his associates shall be in on the discussion of research, development, and production all through the process, and not just at the weapon end.

That is our viewpoint in respect to the section of the law which relates to the liaison with the military: That the information that we are to supply as to our activities is not confined simply to weaponeering, but to the whole operation.

It is an interesting fact that for a Director of Military Application the Commission found a man who was not just a general in the old ironclad tradition—he had been a Rhodes scholar. That looked a little like the expert picking of people they used to do in the Valley.

But you can see that Lilienthal is not going to stand in the way of any general-staff decision to use the product of Los Alamos, and how could he, under the law? He has been known to say that a good administrator can improve a bad law, just as bad administration can ruin a good one; but there is nothing wrong with the McMahon Act except its subject matter. It's a good law, Lilienthal is a good administrator, and the only trouble is that, as the trusted public servant of the American people, he is a man with a load of mischief.

The most you can hope for is that being a man who by inclination was proud of planting a hundred and fifty million trees in the Tennessee Valley, he will do his best to see that radioactivity is used to improve the life of plants and animals, not to wipe both off the face of the globe. He will do better than anybody else at the job, probably, because of the philosophy that says, as his book about TVA puts it, that it is possible to turn calamity into opportunity.

He said, too, in that book that it was "a book about to-morrow," and you can know that he won't want to see all that good work in the Valley go to waste in an atomic war. It isn't even necessary to say of him, as they say of some public men, that he wouldn't want a war because his big tall son, who they say looks just like his father at the same age, would be certain to go with the rest of the young men at Harvard. David Lilienthal has considerations outside his own family, and he knows with other intelligent people that an atomic war wouldn't confine itself to the soldiers.

The alternate to atomic war, as Oak Ridge schoolboys can tell you, is doing something good and useful with atomic power. First on a list of fields to be worked in, according to Dr. Oppenheimer's recommendation to the United Nations Atomic Energy Commission of "the affir-mative advantages of co-operative development," still comes "Atomic energy as an instrument of research and development itself." As an example it is explained that the use of radioactive carbon revolutionizes the scale of research activity, opens up new scientific worlds.

So in talking of exploration to be done in directions not as yet mapped out or even rightly imagined, Lilienthal likes to use the comparison about Columbus, who started out to find a trade route to India. It's a good parallel on several counts, and perhaps the best application is to see how the country now has a chance, perhaps a necessity, to discover itself all over again. If you ever wondered whether Americans born in this country would have the enterprise to do what Columbus did, you now have the opportunity to find out, because the world's biggest adventure is ahead of them.

This sense of adventure Lilienthal got into a speech made during the war, but before the bomb, to the students at New York's City College. There, in the face of world destruction, he outlined great expectations, not of "just rebuilding what the bombs and guns have destroyed," but of new methods applied to farming, new projects of river control that would be "the grand job of our century."

Now this appeal to the adventure sense of young minds on a new and wider scale comes about with the linking of colleges and universities and science foundations over the country into a research network for the Atomic Energy Commission. Corresponding to the tie-up of land-grant colleges with TVA, this new collegiate network has not one, but three centers. Clinton Laboratories at Oak Ridge, through the Oak Ridge Institute of Nuclear Studies, extend the area of co-operation west to the University of Texas. The Argonne National Laboratory, near the University of Chicago, ties in twenty-nine units including Northwestern University and the Mayo Foundation, and runs east to include Carnegie Tech at Pittsburgh. The third center, Brookhaven on Long Island, is operated technically by the Eastern association of universities—Yale, Harvard and Princeton, Columbia, Cornell, Rochester and Pennsylvania, M. I. T. and Johns Hopkins. A fourth center is talked of on the West coast—Los Alamos already works with the University of California.

Oddly, as some would see it, the Lilienthal idea is that this tie-up with universities over the country should provide the grassroots connection that he sees necessary to democratic functioning. He not only wants the people educated, he identifies education with a free people in the way Jefferson did when he proposed to start democratic government with the school ward. As Lilienthal puts it, "It would seem to me that when the people of Iowa, for example, get this new body of knowledge, it should come not from the AEC in Washington but from the University of Iowa, Grinnell College and the whole complex system of local institutions, including the high schools of Des Moines and the grade schools of Sioux City."

People who live near the Brookhaven Laboratory on Long Island have been asking questions to find out whether the laboratory will be a dangerous neighbor, causing baldness and the birth of two-headed calves on near-by farms, or a nuisance interfering with radio reception. In saying "no" the research center is actually conducting grassroots education of the sort Lilienthal has in mind. But the best example is seen in Oak Ridge, where the real miracle was not the building of a "secret city" or even atomic fission, but the production in the first school term after Hiroshima of a group of high-school students capable of discussing the bomb and convincing you that they would be able to cope with the new era.

A man who found time to write a book while directing the country's biggest civilian war job is one who sees practical value in intelligence. After his speech at Lake Success, Lilienthal took a minute off to talk like a Southern farmer and confess his "personal hunch" that research in plant growth and insect control could "repay the people of the United States" for the two and a half billions spent in atomic development. This ties right in with the Muscle Shoals phosphates which, as Lilienthal always said, could be either the key to life or a weapon of death.

For phosphates now read radioactive phosphorus and its use in research—hard to explain to the ordinary citizen, as was the use of phosphate fertilizer, but clear to the scientist and as welcome to him as the fertilizer to the farmer. Lilienthal, who used to keep a chunk of superphosphate on his desk, now carries around uranium bricks to prove that the new material is real.

But you can't be sure even after reading the available literature just what the most useful application of atomic energy will be, because not even the experts know, yet. They are paying a lot of attention to cancer research, and when you think how the small supplies of radium were doled out to hospitals or presented with great ceremony to Madame Curie, you realize that radioactive materials now being produced in impressive quantities at Oak Ridge are ammunition long awaited by the men who fight laboratory battles against disease. Lilienthal says the Commission wants the sort of men who see their technical work in terms of human suffering and its alleviation.

How much hope can we afford to place in scientific salvation? Only in the exhortations of demagogues is the country really distrustful of a "brains trust"; laboratory research as done for the corporations, scientific skill as used in private or public-works engineering, is the practical basis of American life. It should be almost too easy for the general public to accept the optimistic remark of Charles A. Thomas, one of the State Department consultants, who said of atomic energy development that with "industry, the universities and the Government together we will have a three-horse team." It is Lilienthal himself who qualifies this limitless trust in science by mentioning the moral responsibilities of research, and remarking that "When a scientist goes dogmatic, he can make a politician look scientific by comparison."

It is the scientists themselves who now, fortunately, begin to assume the moral responsibilities. They fought for civilian control; they are fighting now to save civilian administration and to avoid that atomic war whose nature they best understand. They are showing a nice care as well for the details of world management. Dr. Henshaw of Oak Ridge, studying Japanese casualties, has suggested that as the fate of Japan "lies much more in the hands of America than most Americans realize," so also "the fate of America will be determined much more by the establishment of policies in Japan than most Americans realize."

That, Southerners can recognize, is a good moral attitude toward reconstruction—one that, adopted earlier by the Yankees, might have saved trouble in the Tennessee Valley. Of course the practical application of such moral considerations is long-term, but the scientists are capable, too, of moving, if not quite fast enough for their new world, at least faster than some other people. As the diplomats at Paris admit failure, the Emergency Committee of Atomic Scientists meets at Princeton to demand what Professor Uréy calls "grassroots" understanding, and what Einstein calls "supra-national" solutions.

Lilienthal belongs with the scientists not because he is himself a scientist but because he is what can be called a scientific or reasonable man. In writing of him you miss the personal crotchets that make it easy to characterize the ordinary, ornery members of the human race. There are no meaningless knobs or unnecessary ornaments or archaic survivals about Lilienthal. In a way it is as hard to describe him as it would be to describe a pane of glass. But it is only through clarity that you can focus scientific vision, in useful applications of man's knowledge. And clarity is now a virtue of the river which used to be muddy but which, as the great boast of the Tennessee Valley Authority, now runs blue.

The absence of mental quirks and emotional blocks makes it possible for Lilienthal to be a "man of parts" in a modern application of the eighteenth-century phrase: he is the sum of the knowledge of the experts with whom he works. His own contribution is to blend their contributions into fluid action.

The reasonableness of mind and evenness of response required for such co-ordination, since they do exist in Lilienthal, constitute arguments for a peaceful world. Although he has survived many battles, he has skillfully avoided more. He doesn't normally antagonize people, doesn't have to in order to do what he wants to do. Because he fights mainly for things that people in general want, he has allies. In work he doesn't fight at all, but gets together a harmonious balanced group; in this way he has regarded both TVA and AEC not as one-man jobs but, as he said of AEC, "a family job."

Of course this phrase is a testimony for Lilienthal family relations, and the stream of visitors to the Lilienthal house at Norris, ranging from TVA people to world celebrities, will testify to the quality of that family group. Mrs. Lilienthal is inclined to think, because she is by nature a quiet person and by resolve a woman who won't try to run her husband's job, that her own efforts go unnoticed. Actually it is plain that she makes the Lilienthal background, as in the Washington office she took the curse off dark walls by hanging yellow curtains and insisting on fresh flowers. When Lilienthal plans a speech the family listen first, and what they don't find understandable goes out. Nancy and nineteen-year-old David both know how to argue with Dad, and with his daughter Lilienthal was, the story goes, once reduced to replying "Listen, now, Nancy, I'm old enough to be your father!"

Just beyond the family orbit come fellow workers as friendly as those neighbors at Norris who, hearing of Truman's reappointment of Lilienthal as chairman of TVA, organized an impromptu parade with the school band and a sound truck to serenade the Lilienthals at 81 Pine Road.

More, people outside the country—all those readers of the many translations of Lilienthal's book—know and trust the man. Jennings Perry has said that all foreigners, seeing an American today, listen anxiously to see if he ticks. But the readers of *TVA: Democracy on the March* know what makes its author tick, and they are not afraid of him.

Because some people tried to make it a handicap, it might as well be noted, too, that David Lilienthal's religious heritage is an asset on the new job. This is a queer thing to say if you know, as those who work with him do, that Lilienthal's religion is the kind—catholic with a small *c*— that enabled him to quote papal encyclicals and develop parallels that won an award from the Catholic Committee of the South, in the same year he preached a sermon to Methodist bishops. Reminiscing about his early years, he told one reporter that he had gone to a Campbellite Sunday school, and the papers made it Carmelite.

But don't forget that eighteen-year-old speech about the dispersed Jewish people, believing in one God and in the brotherhood of man, having as their mission the unifying of the world. Among the people who warned Congress that failure to confirm Lilienthal's nomination would look bad in Europe was William L. Batt, who testified to it at the hearings; Dr. Harry Emerson Fosdick, who said it would be a "national disgrace," and Albert Einstein, who told the radio audience that it would have "grave consequences in international politics." Of these warnings Einstein's carried most weight not only because of his world-wide reputation but because he himself could speak for the scattered people whose pride in and support of Lilienthal is more valuable to world peace than anything a congressman can do. They are a peaceful people, adapting themselves to the ways of the countries in which they live, yet remembering each other and their relationships. When Wendell Willkie flew around the world he stopped in Palestine to talk to Henrietta Szold, the founder of Hadassah, a distant cousin of David Lilienthal. When the Chinese Ambassador, Mr. Hu Shih, visited Norris he mentioned his earlier acquaintance with another Lilienthal cousin in China.

As young David said, thirty years ago, "But how can this people, so few, so scattered, so weak, aid in the unification of the world? We are prone to think in material terms. But this unification of the world is not to be temporal but spiritual. Not with the thunder of cannon nor the ingenuity of diplomacy can the world be brought into a great brotherhood; 'not by the sword but by My spirit, saith the Lord.' Not by the blare of trumpets nor the crash of cymbals shall redemption for the world come, but quietly, through the spirit incarnated in this people. . . ."

In the years that have passed since he said that, fourteen of them—seven lean and seven fat—in the Tennessee Valley, David Lilienthal's style of expressing himself has changed. When he explained to a reporter during the Congressional battle, "I owe this country a lot. Holding down a public job is one way to pay that debt," he reached what is, today, another peak of eloquence. But people who call the man a Communist should remember that these speeches are cut out of the same piece. Lilienthal's idea of public service is tied in with religion and morality; it's a "moral universe," as he put it down in Tennessee, and "What's going on in this valley is definitely ethical."

That is the answer to what Congressional probers kept asking, whether Lilienthal believed in a government of laws or a government of men. Of course he believes in both —men charged with public work should be conscious of a moral responsibility, and the moral fact is the unity of mankind under law. Separating the two is like trying to separate the river and the land.

If you are firm enough in your own principles you can apply them as Lilienthal does, whether he is talking to farmers down in Congressman Rankin's district or to New York liberals at public dinners. All are impressed by a simple, practical approach to public morality which boils down to something like "Democracy is the best policy." This is an unflattering oversimplification of Lilienthal philosophy, as it was of Franklin's, because both men have spoken with real conviction; but both have, as part of the conviction, a sense that policy is important. Its consideration by a politician is also proper, and in fact much less dangerous than failure to consider it.

What Lilienthal shares with Franklin, and both with Jefferson, is an awareness of science as an important factor in politics. In his book Lilienthal noted that dams could be built by Fascists as well as by Democrats; what mattered was how they were used. To the Methodist bishops up in Michigan he said:

As ministers, I need hardly remind you of this: that to the

extent that technology, in business and government, increases and further concentrates the power men wield over their fellow men, it thereby atrophies men's ethical standards, it weakens that respect for the sacredness of human personality without which the concept of man's stewardship to God is rendered empty and meaningless.

The ultrareactionary and the ultraradical both assert that these losses of human values are the inevitable price of technical physical advance. This we deny. But we do not deny that the hazards to the human spirit exist. They are real. We know they are real. No one today can disassociate himself from the spiritual dangers that technology multiplies; not the scientist, nor the administrator, nor the politician, nor the churchman. Nor can we disassociate ourselves, any of us, from every effort to develop methods of administering technology that will magnify, not stultify, the spiritual worth of man. . . .

This problem is at its base a moral issue, and one that is the very stuff of our daily lives. Each day we must meet the test this issue presents—in business dealings, in legislative halls, in union meetings. For in the application of science to men's lives there is a perennial and unremitting conflict between two opposing precepts, that thread their way through every phase of American life: on the one hand the faith in man's stewardship to God as the common father of all of us, and on the other the conflicting concept of power, of the power of men over other human beings. Between these two opposing beliefs we see re-enacted under the fierce and sometimes terrible light of modern science and concentrated political power, the age-old struggle, the struggle between those who would use men as a means of power and those to whom men are the children of God, and therefore not means but ends in themselves.

In this struggle which engages and deeply involves us all it is inspiring to observe our growing impulse to turn to each other for counsel and understanding: administrators, business-men, farmers, workers, scientists, churchmen. It is perhaps a promise and a portent of that integration and wholeness that our fragmented and divided world so desperately needs.

For together we must seek the light and together follow the light, hoping and believing that beyond this night's darkness lies neither destruction nor slavery for the Children of God, but instead that City of freedom and of peace toward which it is man's destiny to strive.

In his sensible application of morality to government Lilienthal most nearly approaches some of the excellent political maxims of Confucius, so that it seems appropriate for Mrs. Lilienthal to hang, as a decoration in the family living room, an "ancestor portrait" which was a present from China. The Chinese maxim which best applies to Lilienthal's career is undoubtedly that one which says "Crisis is opportunity."

To say as some have said that a man who steps forward to help in a crisis is an opportunist, or overambitious, is worse than silly—it can be suicidal. To say that he is rash and overconfident would be more to the point, if he were acting without previous training and experience.

But Lilienthal has the training, and experience has given him also, and rightly, a confidence in what he can do. Bernard Shaw once pointed out that if a man has real intelligence, he must be smart enough to put a proper value on it. If he isn't bright enough to appreciate his own ability, how can it be put to work for the world?

So if, as some say, Lilienthal really wanted the Atomic

Energy Commission job, the world can heave a sigh of re lief and say "Thank God for that." Thank the God of the Campbellites and the Carmelites, and of Confucius, and the God of Israel.

Nowadays it is hard to define God's mercy as they once did, saying that a few just men will save a city. In Lilien thal's office there is, as there should be, a copy of the book called *Hiroshima;* and it may be that there were just men in that place. Nobody can prove it, now.

But in Lilienthal's study at home, among other worn Bibles belonging to the various members of his family, there is the marked one on which he took the oath of office. One of the marked places is the 37th Psalm, "a psalm of David," which says among other things not to fret be cause of evildoers; though the wicked flourish as a green bay tree, the Lord will protect the righteous man, and be his strength. "The steps of a good man are ordered by the Lord."